Y0-AZD-971

Kent Cowgill

BACK IN TIME

**Echoes of a Vanished America
In the Heart of France**

Ibis Press
Paris

> *If you were born around this time or were living and alive, you could feel the old world go and the new one beginning. It was like putting the clock back to when BC became AD. Everybody born around my time was part of both.*
>
> Bob Dylan

> *And so I find that we have descended and degenerated from some far ancestor—some microscopic atom wandering at its pleasure between the mighty horizons of a drop of water perchance—insect by insect, animal by animal, reptile by reptile, down the long highway of smirchless innocence, till we have reached the bottom stage of development—namable as the Human Being. Below us—nothing. Nothing but the Frenchman.*
>
> Mark Twain

Contents

Introduction		9
Chapter 1	"Nasty, Boorish, and Short"	19
Chapter 2	"Navigating *La Rive Gauche*"	29
Chapter 3	"Back In Time"	39
Chapter 4	"Isaiah"	49
Chapter 5	"Bridges"	73
Chapter 6	"Margot"	93
Chapter 7	"Oc"	111
Chapter 8	"Kissing the Gods"	133
Chapter 9	"*Digestif*"	143
Chapter 10	"Frogs"	157
Epilogue		177

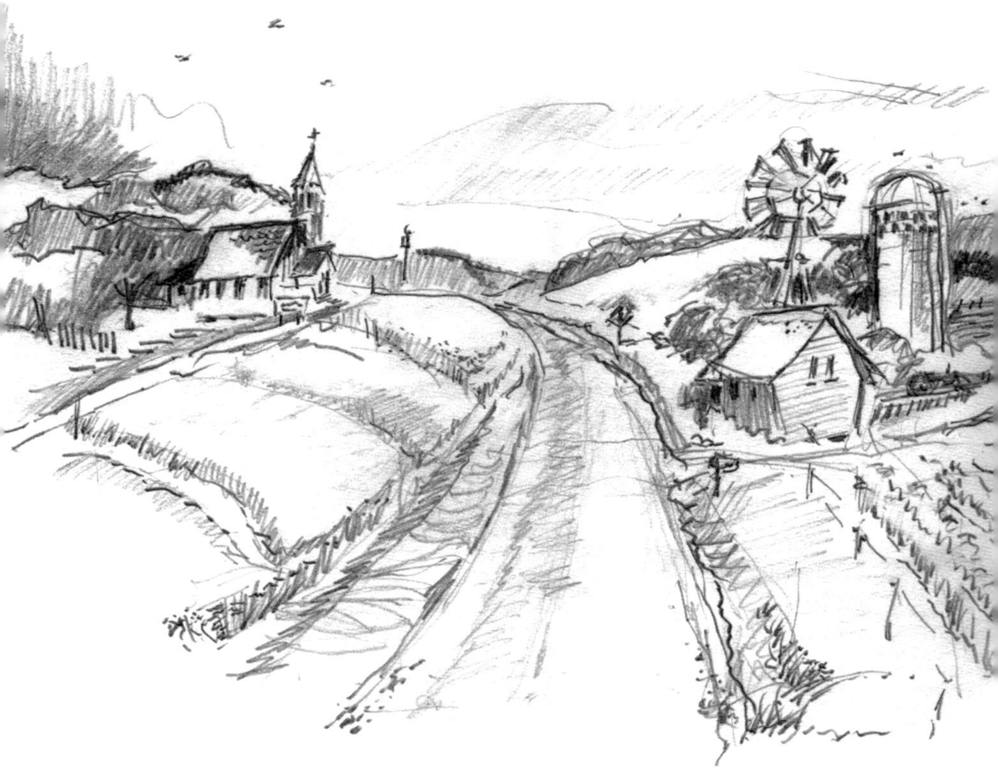

Introduction

To begin, a vivid memory, from so deep in the past it has the surreal coloration of a dream:

It's a brilliant Sunday afternoon, a slanting October sun turning endless rows of corn stalks into golden ingots, and the family Packard has rolled to a dusty stop on a country road in the heart of the Plains. I jump out of the back, jamming three shotgun shells into my sixteen-gauge pump as my mother hurriedly cranks down her front-seat window. She is wearing a fringed deerskin jacket, a head scarf, and a worn pair of jodhpurs tucked into hunting boots laced to the knees. As I pass her I hear the clatter of her own gun emerging from the opened window, the metallic click of a single shell locked into place.

Behind the steering wheel, my father waits as I hop up and straddle the right front fender. His twelve-gauge remains in the back seat, propped between my two younger brothers, and will be used only if the next few volatile seconds allow sufficient time. I know the first volley will echo from my own gun, loaded and ready, my thumb poised above the safety and my feet primed to hit the road once the car brakes again to a lurching stop. My heart beats faster with anticipation—the moment when the engine dies in a spray of gravel and I spring off on the shoulder, taking care only to stay clear of the protruding barrel of my mother's four-ten. For just as suddenly the flush will come, out of the weedy ditch where the bird had disappeared crossing the road half a minute earlier—the cock pheasant exploding into the azure sky in startled cackles and streaming hues of vermilion and white and blue…

We called it "road hunting," and from early childhood to the day I left for college, it was the climax of countless autumn weekends played out over the hundred miles that separated my grandmother's rustic house in Guide Rock, on the north bank of the Republican

River in southern Nebraska, from the even tinier village of Silver Creek that was our home. Almost none of it seemed dreamlike, or even faintly anachronistic, back then. I knew my grandmother had been born the year Custer died at the Little Bighorn. That her ramshackle barn where we played cowboys and Indians held a rusted Civil War bayonet and a broken-wheeled, cracked leather buggy. That Jesse James and his brother Frank—so at least she claimed to the day she died at age one hundred—had taken shelter in her widowed mother's homestead one stormy evening during her own childhood, leaving twenty dollars in gold coins on the kitchen table after taking turns standing watch through the night with their pistols drawn. Such shadowy presences alone whispered of a vanished past, not the creaking pump behind the back step where we drew our water, nor the hand-crank, party-line telephone with its two-digit number, or the canvas-curtained screen porch where my brothers and I slept regardless of the season, buried under a mound of tattered quilts against the knifing prairie wind.

Within those lodestars of permanence, the autumn hunting weekends became an acute, almost painful introduction to the evanescence of time—forty-eight fleeting hours that built from our fervent anticipation of my father's arrival home from work late Friday to the deflating moment the old Packard coughed to a stop back in our cluttered garage on Sunday night. The events between were as fixed and invariable as the ticking of a clock. Saturday morning meant rising before dawn to hunt or fish on the river—then a return at ten to wolf down my grandmother's jam-slathered graham pancakes and clean whatever game we had killed. Afternoon meant football—listening to our beloved, maddeningly mediocre Cornhuskers on the ancient Motorola in the parlor, then playing our own rowdy games of tackle on the leaf or snow covered lawn. When darkness drove us back indoors we sat down to feast once more, this time on whatever we had shot or caught or harvested earlier in the summer from the vegetable garden—the day's bounty of duck, pheasant, quail, or catfish garnished with Mason jars of produce toted up from the dank, cobwebby depths of the storm cellar by the back door. Dominoes and Chinese checkers filled the shank of the evening, until my father turned down the fire in the parlor stove and we sank wearily into our feather beds.

Yet it was Sunday, always, that stamped the march of time's indissoluble mix of joy and melancholy on my soul. *Sun day.* I don't know how old I was when I first made the conscious connection between the glowing orb's inexorable advance across the heavens and the intensity of emotion those too brief autumn weekends stirred in me. I do remember that the thrills of the homeward road-hunts were heightened, in a prologue almost physically unbearable, by two creeping hours of church worship so inviolable in family tradition I had collected fourteen consecutive year-bars for perfect attendance before I finally missed a service, shortly after I graduated from high school, at eighteen. What stand out now are the hymns—our earnest warblings of "Bringing In The Sheaves," "Blessed Assurance," "When The Roll Is Called Up Yonder"—and the gaunt, arm-flailing preacher's hellfire and damnation sermons on the imminent Apocalypse. Like my own parents, he and his eerily pale-skinned wife had three children whose conception I found impossible to conceive—a wondrously devout trio of whom I knew little beyond the awe-inspiring fact that their names were all Biblical and that the oldest, following in his father's footsteps, had recently taken orders at the Moody Bible Institute in Chicago and been sent off as a missionary to convert the heathen natives in Rome.

I look back at it all now from a vastly different America, one in which a far more powerful Republican river has widened to the breaking point the breach between that deeply cherished past and the rural culture I still call home. A few weeks after the last Presidential election, at a family reunion near that same turbid little watercourse where I'd spent so many idyllic hours in willow-shrouded duck blinds and fishing holes during my youth, I was approached by a California cousin who had long since drifted away, as I had, from those distant roots. "You know why it's called the Republican, don't you?" he whispered, one eye cocked sardonically toward a great-uncle holding forth on the Satanic evils of anti-war kooks and gay marriage. A long, penetrating pause followed. "Because it's shallow," he answered, "it's crooked, and it's clogged with dirt."

I hadn't become quite that disillusioned, but the bitter joke was a poignant reminder of how far away the past seemed. The breach felt even wider, and sadly ironic, because I retained so many of the mental markers that should have kept me firmly grounded in the political party almost as entrenched in family history as the evangelical church. I preferred living in the country to the city, remained an avid outdoorsman, believed firmly in rugged independence, individual responsibility, and whatever "moral values" were repulsed by self-absorbed materialism and the culture's steady drift toward once-unimaginable levels of smut and sleaze. So deeply rooted had been my childhood in the G.O.P. my first published writing was a florid bit of doggerel in praise of General Eisenhower, whose hand I had shaken at a Kansas campaign rally just before the 1952 election, when I was ten. My family had spent that election eve clustered around the radio in the same turreted old Victorian house that my ninety-one-year old mother and I had returned to for the reunion, almost literally a stone's throw from the aptly named river. The spasm of fear I'd felt at a great-aunt's sudden shriek of horror on that long ago night was another indelible childhood memory—her prophesies of doom if Adlai Stevenson, "that Red Communist," were to hold the lead the early returns indicated he'd built in the East.

That particular aunt was a card-carrying member of the Daughters of the American Revolution who even back then, half a century ago, had struck my callow eyes as bordering on the lunatic fringe. It had taken far longer to reach the painful distance that had opened between my current life and the less extreme but still stanch Republican loyalties of my more immediate family, a reflexive allegiance that crystallized in another vivid memory. Through nearly all those years of my childhood—the hundreds of weekends spent in my grandmother's spartan little home before she finally consented, well into her eighties, to the installation of indoor plumbing—it was my job to tote the family chamber pot out to the outhouse every morning. The malodorous bucket was unfailingly referred to as "the Democrat," or more often, simply as "the Demo." I was at least thirteen before it dawned on me the term wasn't its universal name.

That latest family reunion had ended early Sunday afternoon, and at her request, I drove my mother back to Silver Creek on the same dusty country roads we had hunted all those years before, past fence-to-fence, wind-whipped corn fields whose pivot-irrigation pipes lay stacked where shelterbelts and thorny groves of hedge orange had once flourished—past denuded ditches that had once teemed with quail and pheasants, land where even the remnants of rotting barns and abandoned houses had been burned off or plowed under to create still more featureless acres for genetically-engineered corn the nation needed only if corn-based ethanol and prime beef retained their reflexive grip on our perceived needs. Truckloads of it rose in swelling hills beside the overstuffed grain elevators of the tiny, faded villages whose names still held for me more than a trace of their old magic. *Red Cloud*, barely a dozen miles from my grandmother's house in Guide Rock—the childhood home of Willa Cather. *Blue Hill. Ayr. Eldorado. Harvard.* And finally *Clarks*, where my other set of grandparents had lived, ten miles up Highway 30 from Silver Creek. "All photographs," Susan Sontag pointedly observed, "are *memento mori*." Driving slowly through my hometown's vacant streets in the autumn dusk, I felt the same keen awareness that all memories are too. It was impossible to block out the decline in these once-vibrant villages, or to suppress the sense of loss.

Aside from its remote location a stone's throw from the Kansas state line, Guide Rock, Nebraska had been a more or less typical prairie hamlet back then. Though it boasted no more than six hundred residents, the small farms on its outskirts supported two thriving grocery stores, a movie theater and a dance hall, and close to twenty other small businesses that bloomed with life when the farmers hit town on Saturday night, and then again, more quietly, to fill its three steepled churches on Sunday morning. Through the following decades of atrophy, as the rural economy increasingly fell into a mad spiral of ever-larger farms, subsidized overproduction, and depressed prices for those piled mountains of excess grain, the once-thriving village, like so many others on the Plains, had taken on the cadaverous look of an aging drug addict. The image felt as inevitable as the tragic reality—the exploding number of methamphetamine labs that had scourged the state in recent years.

Guide Rock had been my mother's home until she was twenty, and as we left the reunion in Superior, she asked me to take "the river road" back to it as we'd so often done over the years. I gladly did so—felt my spirits lift briefly as the winding strip of gravel led us past chokecherry-fringed ditches and silvery stands of cottonwood that had somehow escaped the relentless pressure for still more acres of tillable land. The drift back in time died the moment we reached the village and stopped briefly on the bridge to stare down at the river, so diminished by irrigation only an ankle-deep trickle flowed where it had often run five or six feet deep during my youth. We crept on down Main Street, toward the high school, where a lifesize statue of an infantryman honoring those who had died in the First World War had stood proudly erect during my childhood. The statue remained where it had always stood, but the school was gone. Its tax base and rural student body depleted by the shrunken population, it had joined thousands of others similarly demolished or permanently shuttered across the Plains.

A few months before, on the phone with an old college friend who had recently suffered a heart attack his doctor had cautioned him was brought on by the stress of farming, I'd asked him what it was like, the life of a small farmer today. As a former president of The Nebraska Wheatgrowers Association who also raised corn and soybeans, Ed was a man I had long admired and trusted, and I was curious what his take would be on the divisive issues that had made twenty-first-century agriculture a battleground of conflicting information and special interests. It would take another year for the international wrangling over farm subsidies and tariffs to reach the level of discord that threatened the December, 2005 WTO summit in Hong Kong, but the problems triggering it were already clear.

"Start with the definition of 'small farmer'", Ed answered my question. "My son and I are currently working 2500 acres. Not that long ago, it would have been considered a fairly large farm out here. Now it's barely enough to support a single household. And with the rising price of fuel, it won't be long before your 'small farm' will have to be even bigger than that.

"Everything has gotten bigger," he went on. "The debt you carry, the size of the equipment, the amount of fertilizer you've got to use. Twelve-row corn planters are as common now as four-rows were back when I started out with my father. You see three-hundred-horse John Deeres or Caterpillars working ground where you used to see a sixty or seventy horse Farmall. When I got out of college, we'd top-dress a little dry fertilizer on the sandy hills. Now we use starter and thirty pounds per acre of nitrogen on our wheat—over forty pounds of chemicals total—and sixty on the corn. Weed control back then was mostly tillage, maybe a little 2-4D on the worst places. Today it's herbicides and pesticides on every acre you own."

The picture he painted was dispiriting enough I asked again about his health. He was doing fine, he reassured me. He was more concerned about his son, not yet forty, who had recently been put on his own regimen of heart medication. But hell, he grunted, he was a farmer. "There's only so much you can do to cut back and still make a go of it. The work's got to be done."

The grim reminder of the precariousness of farm life was sobering, and before I wished him the best and hung up I asked him one thing more.

"A cousin of mine lives in Superior," I told him, "the next town up the road from Guide Rock, where I spent a lot of time back in the day. He's so concerned about methamphetamine use in the county he helped organize a series of town hall meetings to address it. They struck a loud enough chord the story was eventually picked up by *The New York Times*."

"I hadn't heard about that," my friend responded, "but meth is a big problem back here, no question. My neighbor got killed four years ago by a guy who made the stuff, in an abandoned house less than three miles up the road."

The story stunned me, despite what my cousin had reported and the obvious fact that rural poverty and despair were a perfect breeding ground for both the makeshift labs and the increased local addictions that had inevitably followed in their wake. I'd read the *Times* article after my cousin told me of it—discovered that Nebraska had some of the statistically poorest counties in the United States.

"It's not hard to make," Ed spoke into the ensuing silence. "You can't drive ten miles in Nebraska without passing a tank of anhydrous ammonia. All they have to do is show up during the night with a container and bleed out whatever they need."

Driving home to Minnesota after the reunion, I tried to come to grips with all of it, in the wake of an election that had left America more bitterly divided than it had been since the Vietnam War. In the wee hours of election morning, I had stood in an airport rain twenty miles from my house and shaken the losing candidate's hand after the last stop of his exhaustive, irreparably flawed campaign. Though I'd spent two afternoons the previous week working to get out the vote for him, the impact when he lost was less sadness or anger than a numbed dismay at the pundits' consensus opinion that a deciding issue had been "family values"–the potent mix of "faith-based" religion, militant morality, and unquestioning, knee-jerk patriotism that was as incomprehensible as the fact it had become so dominant in the rural heartland where I'd lived since birth. My youth had been shaped by a form of all three, but both the term and the "values" it celebrated felt weirdly, even tragically distorted. The countless church services I'd dutifully attended were as apolitical as the quietly murmured Lord's Prayer for universal tolerance and brotherhood that concluded them; there was only a needling humor, no venom, in my folks' allusions to the chamberpot "Demo"; and if I ever heard anyone voice an audible word on the values of the family, it was a passing reference to the Golden Rule or the importance of passing a bond issue for improvements to the local school.

I knew many of the changes were inevitable, the result of passing time. But some weren't, or didn't feel like they were. The blind trust in political snake-oil salesmen and right-wing demagogues willing to use any lie or distortion to advance their self-serving agendas. The smug contempt for other nations appalled by our cultural arrogance and gunslinging adventurism. An uncritical swallowing of saccharine pledges like "No child left behind" and "compassionate conservatism," glitzy euphemisms that sanitized the kind of appalling social injustice only the willfully ignorant or overtly racist had once condoned. And most of all, the astonishing disregard for mountains of scientific evidence on the increasingly perilous condition of the planet—the once sacred water and land. In those glum days following the election, all of it left me feeling like some aging Huckleberry Finn, yearning to light out for a different Territory. I knew the people of the Plains were decent and hard-working—far more victims than agents of the forces that had transformed their culture—and that a number of vibrant small farms and villages remained. But I needed space, if only temporarily, to get a more distanced perspective in a rural culture that still felt timeless and familiar. A week after I returned from the reunion, I bought a plane ticket to France.

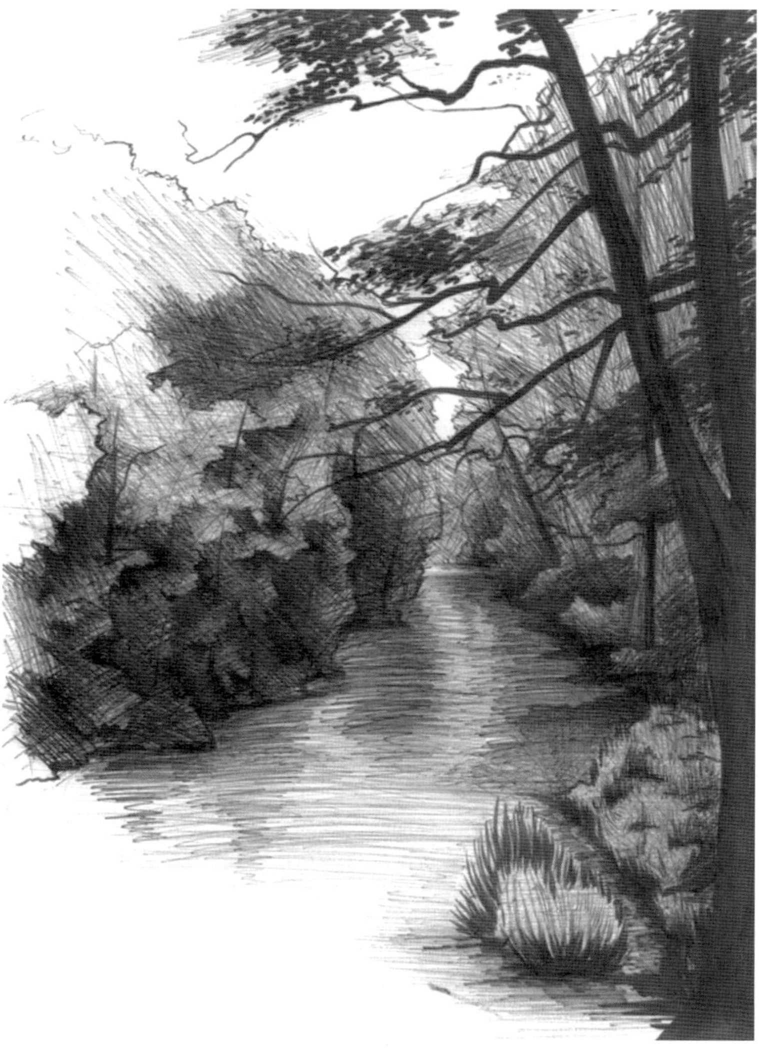

Chapter 1
Nasty, Boorish, and Short

The French were rude. The French were arrogant. They were so tight their asses squeaked and so self-absorbed the sound was music to their ears. Above all, the French were cowards. "Y'hear about that French rifle for sale on eBay?" I'd overheard a ruddy-faced wit ask the clerk in my local hardware store in the heady days after U.S. troops occupied Baghdad. "Dropped once. Never been fired."

I'd heard the stereotypes as far back as I could remember, and read them too. Most had been part of the American mainstream long before the invention of Freedom Fries. Among countless examples, there was this typically acerbic barb by Mark Twain: "We look upon rabbits as being weak, but what is the meekness of the rabbit to the meekness of the Frenchman?" The stigmas were hardly limited to my own heartland culture. Struggling to file a lost luggage claim at DeGaulle airport a few years earlier, I'd had ample opportunity to ponder George Orwell's portrait of a "nasty, sour-faced, interfering little man" who was "the typical French official." Even my wife nodded knowingly at that one, still stung by the distant memory of a churlish ticket agent who had greeted her on her first visit to Paris with "Ah yes, ze young woman who thinks she can speak French."

Not yet retired from a college teaching career, as I was, Jane would not be lighting out with me to the City of Light on this occasion, even if she were inclined to. But when I told her of my impulsive decision, she was loving, or at least charitable, enough to smile grimly and wish me well. To several acquaintances less familiar with my eccentricities, however, word that I was about to spend six weeks in France in the dead of winter brought the same look to their faces a Jehovah's Witness must see when he raps on somebody's door. Whether they had once been snubbed by a waiter on the Champs Elysée or never ventured east of Chicago, the point of view was unmistakable, if mostly implied rather than stated: for any red-blooded American, the snooty little nation across the Atlantic was about as bad as it got.

Long schooled myself in rural Minnesotan, I said little in response—didn't tell them that my France was different. I mumbled only that I hadn't found the negative stereotypes to be very accurate, aside from the occasional Orwellian bureaucrat, even in Paris. Said nothing at all about the *campagne*, where on half a dozen previous trips over a quarter of a century I'd discovered a country filled with the kind of rustic villages and family-owned hotel-restaurants that had all but vanished from the United States. In memory, that France felt like this:

You descend a worn wooden stair from your *Logi*'s cramped but tidy quarters to the dining room at the appointed hour, sometime between seven and nine-thirty in the evening. The hostess, typically the owner with her chef husband, greets you with a nod or a few formal words of welcome, then leads you to a quiet table where a fresh-cut flower blooms in a discreet glass vase. There is no background music—no background anything—unless two or three tasteful but unobtrusive paintings or photos hung on the drab papered walls qualify as background. A handful of other tables in the room are also occupied by diners of varied ages, unmistakably French in their subdued shades of brown and gray. You nod to them and exchange polite once-overs as you're seated, mumble the de rigueur "*bonsoir*"s. From that moment on, as you bend for the next hour over food so unpretentiously delicious you can think of little else but the pleasure of eating, no sound rises above the faint clink of a knife or fork against glassware, the unhurried flow of quiet footsteps as the hostess or a demure young waitress carries another much-gazed-at dish into the softly lit room. The church-like silence continues through a culminating *crème brulée* or *tarte tatin* and a steaming cup of coffee or espresso—maybe a *digestif* which you sip slowly, stretching your limbs contentedly away from the mostly uneaten dessert cheese. An older couple across the room exchange nods with you for the third or fourth time, smiling knowingly. Minutes more pass as additional sips of the cognac burn satisfyingly in your throat. And then it happens, with the magical suddenness of a hummingbird arriving to hold in a motionless whir over a delicate blossom. A conversation begins, a few murmured words as decorous as those exchanged at a gravesite. Then someone at an adjacent table speaks as well, perhaps another, until the little room somehow remains serenely peaceful yet pulses with a shared, glowing life. No matter how minimal or mangled your French, your fellow diners are warmly complimentary: "*Non, monsieur, au contraire, votre français est très bon!*"

It was that France I wanted to return to. Rural. Salt-of-the-earth. Provincial. A place where those words still held largely positive connotations, not the flag-waving xenophobia and religious fanatacism they'd too often come to have in the United States. Though it was an absurd season for travel, I'd yielded to the impulse to leave soon—as soon as I could get the decks cleared—for both the badly needed physical and mental distance and the gut-level feeling that *that France* wouldn't be there forever. My last visit, four years earlier, had seen noticeably more Golden Arches, not as many *artisan boulangeries* with their golden sheaf of wheat discreetly painted above the bakery's front door. The little hotel-restaurants remained, but fewer of them too, with more unmistakable signs on every visit that the Wal-Marting of a country was an economic phenomenon to which not even the French were immune. How much more had changed since I'd last been there? The longer I thought about the trip in the days after I bought the plane ticket and leased a rental car, the more problematic it began to seem. Had my mind been momentarily clouded by the dispiriting election—by a family reunion and a wistful return to old haunts that swept me back to a long-vanished era? Would my outsider's view of a foreign nation that was almost obsessively distrusted, even despised, by an apparent majority of my countrymen hold up under a more penetrating gaze?

I had fallen hard for France almost before I knew the country existed, smitten first by professional hockey games beamed in faint radio waves across the cornbelt from dimly imagined arenas in Chicago and Detroit. What transfixed me were the players' names. *André Pronovost. Maurice "the Rocket" Richard. Henri Richard, "the Pocket Rocket,"* his little brother. Collectively they were known as "the flying Frenchmen," the "*habitants*" of the perennial monarchs of hockey, the Montreal Canadiens, their stylish dash and verve on the ice accented by the colors of their uniforms, which the announcers occasionally referred to as the "*bleu, blanc, et rouge.*" The broadcasts were in English, but the players' mesmerizing French-Canadian monikers were not, though I had no idea how to spell them. The dichotomy was a continuing source of bafflement that left me convulsed with laughter, years later, when I read a *Sports Illustrated* article on the Quebecois All-Star Rod Gilbert, whose fan mail from that generation's hero-worshipping kids was sometimes addressed simply to "Roger Bear, New York Rangers."

The first dim light hadn't dawned for me until I was nine or ten—a spring morning when the *Omaha World-Herald* sports section that I devoured daily ran a story on the climactic game of the Stanley Cup finals, where the *On-ree Ree-char* whose radio exploits had so dazzled me was exposed as the diminutive "Henry Richard." In that mind-bending moment, the fairy dust of the French language was sprinkled over me forever, to the point I spent hours contemplating the changes in my own life if I'd been lucky enough to be born with such a mellifluous handle. *Kent Cow-gill* clearly didn't cut it, especially after I learned from my father that a literal translation of the last was "Cattle Crossing." Even when I French-kissed it to *Kent Co-ZHEE*, as I often did in my mind, it still fell woefully short of *Jean Beliveau* or *Bernard Andre "Boom Boom" Geoffrion*.

If such bittersweet experiences shaped my early, entirely secret feelings about a land no one in my immediate world of experience seemed much to like or respect, things only got knottier as I grew older. Needing a foreign language to complete the requirements for a graduate degree, I chose French without hesitation, plunging headlong into a semester of intensive five-class-a-week study. The course proved effective enough I was able to pass the requisite exam when it ended. Unfortunately, since only a reading knowledge of the language was required, the professor had devoted no time at all to speech or pronunciation. The experience left me with an even more acute case of francophilia—and led directly, not long after I finally set foot on French soil a decade later, to one of the most embarrassing incidents of my life.

I was married to my first wife back then, and a tailpipe had given out on the camping van we'd driven into the vine-covered hills of Burgundy. Nursing the rasping vehicle on to the next village, we'd finally found a grease-stained mechanic who rubbed his chin appraisingly and grunted that, *bien sûr, monsieur,* he could do the repair work. Mutually at a loss for things to say as he put the vehicle on a hoist and hunched his broad frame under it, the two of us passed several awkward minutes exchanging more cryptic grunts and snatches of *franglais* before somehow stumbling on the subject of trout fishing, which he seemed to love as much as I. *Oui*, he eventually managed to convey through an escalating mélange of words and gestures, *les petites rivières* in the region indeed held *beaucoup de truites.* The tragedy was, *dommage,* his work permitted him only one or two days a month to fish them. Shaking his head morosely, he asked if I got out much. Or at least that's what I deduced he had asked me from the flow of alien syllables and the spincasting motion he made with the ruined tailpipe in his hand. "*Absolument*," I responded immediately—the streams where I lived back in America also held a lot of fish, though I typically used flies to catch them. Seeing his brow furrow in confusion, I repeated the last phrase—"*Je pêche avec la bouche*"—this time adding my own mimed imitation of delivering a feathered hook to an imaginary pool under the pinup nude calendar on the far wall. It was at least an hour later, and fifty kilometers down the road, when the realization hit me. The word for fly was *la mouche,* not *la bouche.* I'd told him I fished with my mouth. Several numb minutes farther on, his glassy-eyed expression still looming in front of me, the second bombshell detonated. *Pêcher* was one of those fiendish French verbs that did double duty. The way I had accented it, what I'd actually said was "I sin with my mouth."

I don't know how long it took that mute garageman to recover from the experience, only that even now I occasionally wonder what he told his own wife at the dinner table that night. It's possible he's still swearing to her that he once met this weird American who made wild, jerking motions with his right fist while crowing about the oral perversions he performed on brown trout.

My past held enough such humbling cross-cultural encounters I'd learned at least two things about the daunting country I was going to spend six winter weeks in. The first was the full resonance of a line I'd once seen in a book by P.G. Wodehouse, which in memory read "He had that glum, hangdog look of an Englishman about to speak French." The second was that most of what my own countrymen seemed to believe about the insufferably rude and arrogant Frogs was about as reliable as accounts of ten-foot alligators in the sewers of New York.

Still, maybe inevitably, the negative stereotypes gnawed at the edges of my psyche. What had begun simply as an angst-ridden, escapist whim had slowly morphed into a whole set of troubling questions I couldn't suppress. What if my skeptical friends were right—that a lifetime of francophilia had led me to turn a blind eye on anything that didn't fit my idealized image of French culture? Had my half-dozen previous sojourns through the country been too superficial to mean anything? And most unsettling of all, had the fallout from Iraq and Abu Ghraib and other recent tragic debacles turned the good will I'd always experienced into something closer to the opposite, an antipathy toward anyone whose passport read "*The United States.*" In the stunned and grieving days after 9/11, the French newspaper *Le Monde* had run a front-page editorial avowing "*Nous sommes tous Américains,*" an expression of national empathy that had faded so completely a *New Yorker* columnist could credibly write, barely three years later, of a growing apprehension "that the anti-Bush sentiments manifest throughout much of the world will now transmute into fully fledged anti-Americanism." Could such a transmutation have occurred even in the secluded French villages where I'd felt so welcome, bucolic outposts whose gentle rhythms I had come to think of almost as my own?

The longer I considered them, the more I had to acknowledge that I didn't know the answers to any of these questions. I knew only that the trip had become something very different from the blithe meanderings of my previous visits, and that I wanted, even needed, more from the country I had admired for so long. Whatever I was about to experience might remain fool's gold, a tourist's image of truth, but I was determined to get beyond the "*Ça va?*"s and "*de rien*"s that greased the Gallic social wheels the way "How's it goin'?"

and "Have a nice day" did the rural culture I lived in. I wanted to touch the heart of provincial France and see if it beat the way I'd long believed it did, and whether that quiet pulsebeat still felt like the American heartland I'd once inhabited. And there was one thing more. I knew all too much about what my country thought about the French. What I didn't know was what the French, deep down, thought about us.

Nearly a half-century earlier, as chronicled in his road narrative *Travels With Charley*, John Steinbeck had set off on his own search for a nation's soul in the weeks just prior to the watershed Nixon-Kennedy election. His trip began, as mine would, from the conviction that "New York is no more America than Paris is France or London is England." And to the extent that a cattleman from Kansas inhabited different psychic terrain from a Hollywood hairdresser that truth about America still clearly held. There was another profound sense, however, in which the urban/rural divide didn't seem to hold even in Steinbeck's time, as his book's subsequent chapters make increasingly evident. For even back then, the Burger Kinging and Dairy Queening of the country was as imminent in the hinterlands as anywhere else:

"*In the eating places along the roads the food has been clean, tasteless, colorless, and of a complete sameness. It is almost as though the customers had no interest in what they ate as long as it had no character to embarrass them.... Now and then I would see a sign that said 'home-made sausage' or 'home-smoked bacon and hams' or 'new-laid eggs' and I'd stop to lay in supplies. Then, cooking my own breakfast and making my own coffee, I found that the difference was instantly apparent. A freshly laid egg does not taste remotely like the pale, battery-produced refrigerated egg. The sausage would be sweet and sharp and pungent with spices, and my coffee a wine-dark happiness. Can I then say that the America I saw has put cleanliness first, at the expense of taste? And—since all our perceptive nerve trunks including that of taste are not only perfectible but also capable of trauma—that the sense of taste tends to disappear and that strong, pungent, or exotic flavors arouse suspicion and dislike and so are eliminated?*"

Over the years, I had fallen under the hypnotic spell of what the French called *la France profonde* primarily because its strong and pungent flavors had not perished. They lived on in every town market, farm-made pâte, and midday game of *boules* lazily unfolding under leafy plain trees in village squares. The astonishing thing to me, re-reading Steinbeck's book shortly before my departure, was not that these colorful ingredients of rural life had largely vanished from our culture as far back as 1960. That fact squared all too painfully with my own memories, for I had grown up witnessing the change. What stunned me was his broader point—that the loss of those distinctive flavors in rural America was less an indictment of our culinary sins than of our political culture. Talking to people throughout the country, he claimed to have found scarcely anyone willing to voice a strong opinion on the upcoming, soon to be historic election. Reading him in the immediate aftermath of the most venomous Presidential race of my lifetime, I found myself in the pointedly ironic position of deploring this more recent country flavor—an America where nearly everyone had, and seemed all too willing to express, political opinions that often seemed appallingly oblivious of the facts.

Considering the matter further, I wondered if part of our knee-jerk scorn for the sometimes insufferably proud nation across the Atlantic could have arisen from a vague sense of jealous loss—the realization, however faint and defensive, that those more satisfying flavors still existed in its rural villages and small towns. I had built a tentative trip itinerary around six of them, which I'd chosen both for their regional diversity and an array of fondly remembered experiences I'd had there in the past. Arromanches-les-Bains, on the coast of Normandy, sat at the heart of the D-Day invasion beaches. Souillac, in the Dordogne, had a sublime Romanesque church and a seedy bar where I'd bibulously joined in raucous celebration of France's dramatic World Cup soccer victory in 1998. A hundred kilometers farther south, the larger town of Cahors beckoned for its jet-dark wine, the best farmer's market I'd ever strolled through, and rugged terrain hauntingly similar to the wooded bluffs along the upper Mississippi River near my Minnesota home.

My fourth and fifth target destinations were in Languedoc, the topographically varied province of southwest France which on a sabbatical leave with Jane in the mid-90's had become my favorite part of the country. Montpeyroux was a tiny village enclosed by vineyards that took me back to the corn-encircled hamlets of my childhood—a sleepy island in the stream of time where a cluttered little family store sold everything from bottled gas to fresh *chèvre* and a cantankerous old tom turkey gobbled threateningly whenever I passed his front-yard pen. A few kilometers up the Hérault valley perched the even tinier village of St. Guilhem le Désert, where I'd once experienced a moment that came as close as any in my life to feeling spiritual. And finally, I set my sights on the tiniest of them all, a hilltop three-*chambre* hôtel-restaurant so far off the beaten path it was difficult to imagine, when Jane and I and two traveling companions had stumbled on it three years later in Burgundy, that such a place could still be.

There were countless other villages and towns I could have chosen, but I settled on this otherwise dissimilar set of six because they promised an especially varied fusion of the two psychological currents that had generated the trip: escapist flight—the compulsion to light out for territory I deeply wanted to believe still existed despite the seismic changes that had transformed my own rural culture—and the perhaps equally quixotic hope of learning how everyday French people, people like those I grew up with and continued to live among, viewed us from their distant vantage point across the sea. Hyperpatriotism, sports, concerns over declining values, a world-view rigidly shaped by religion—they were the driving engines of the rural America I lived in, and I hoped to discover how they resonated in places I had come to love almost as much as the villages of my childhood but that I *knew*, if I were honest with myself, scarcely at all. Like jewels on a string, the six formed a loop around the center of the country, north to south from Paris and then back again. Whatever I was destined to find in them, I'd packed a notebook and a small tape recorder to chronicle it. In this state of anticipation and uncertainty I set off at the end of January. The temperature when my flight landed in Paris, ten hours later, was lower than it had been in Minneapolis when I boarded the plane.

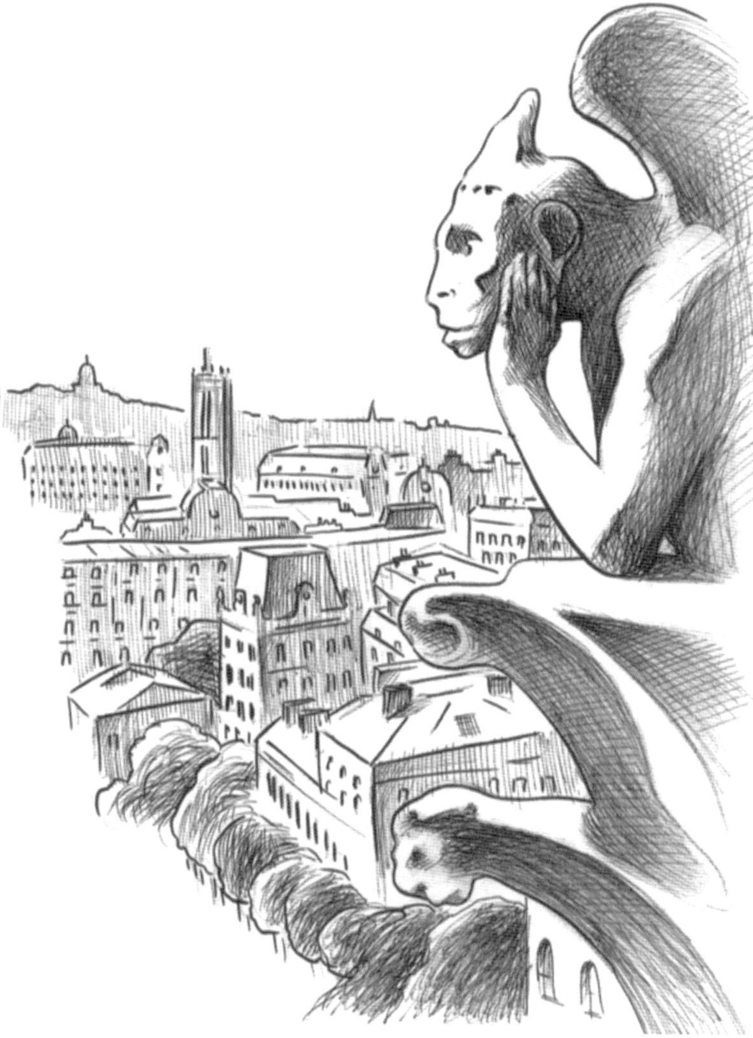

Chapter 2
Navigating *La Rive Gauche*

Paris remained the loveliest city I knew, even in the dismal weather, and on the cab ride in from the airport I was already glad I'd belatedly booked four nights in an inexpensive little hotel just off the Place des Vosges. I'd come to France for its *campagne*, the bucolic country beyond the Ile de France, had given little thought to this lingering stopover in the metropolis beyond some soul-nurturing indulgence in its peerless restaurants and art galleries. It would have startled me to learn I was about to take a pair of headlong leaps into the murky waters of Franco-American relations, one an experience destined to color the rest of the trip.

The first occurred minutes after I checked into the hotel, when, jet-lagged and famished, I walked distractedly into a seductively lit little Basque bistro just up the street. It was seven o'clock in the evening. My mind was absorbed with food and sleep, in that order—both as soon as possible. And seconds after I opened the curtained door I realized I'd just committed the kind of gaffe that marked me instantly as a *plouc*—the French vernacular for hick—or worse, as the stereotypical ugly American. Three men sat staring coldly at me, all wearing white aprons. Plates of food filled the table in front of them. The silence, once the clatter of the flung-open door subsided, engulfed me like a cannon's roar.

I had been away from France too long, my sea legs not yet under me. Yet a string of facts abruptly registered in the next awkward seconds: the cardboard clock face on the door had read *nineteen-thirty*; a French restaurant's staff ate their own meals in the hour before it opened; I had just violated a space only slightly less private than the dinner table of one's home.

The experience wasn't unfamiliar to me. As a terminally dazzled Francophile from the American hinterlands, I'd learned long ago that *gay Pah-ree* and *les gaucheries* form an inevitable rhyme in French. The blunder I'd just committed, in fact, would scarcely have registered on the Richter scale of my previous linguistic indiscretions—the *bouche/mouche* fault lines that still sent tremors through my soul. Where the sanctities of the French language were concerned, I'd sinned with my mouth at least as often as Inspector Clouseau.

The three men said nothing as I continued to stare mutely at them. Regaining my bearings, I forced a chagrined smile and blurted the requisite apologies, long since become reflexive from frequent use: "*Pardon, messieurs*"..."*Je vous dérange*"..."*Je suis désolé.*" And with the suddenness of quicksilver, the frost vanished from the room. When I returned an hour later, still flushed with embarrassment but even hungrier, the amused *patron* led me to a cozy corner table as if I were a favored client, and the waiter indulged me with a hospitality as warmly attentive as the chef's food was superb.

The second incident was more complicated, a less public yet far more brazen plunge into the capricious currents of Franco-American rapport. Three weeks earlier, back in Minnesota, a friend had lent me a recently published book on fly-fishing along the 41st parallel—a vivid description of several remote and exotic sites around the world. The most absorbing chapter described a Parisian named Pierre Affre, whose adventurous life and angling exploits grew more intriguing with every page I turned. The writer mentioned in passing a Paris address—an office on the *rue Dauphine*—and on a whim I dashed off a short letter to Monsieur Affre mentioning my own angling background and asking if we could meet.

When a return email arrived a week later, I was both surprised and delighted, and more delighted still that it included the Frenchman's cell phone number and an invitation to call him once I'd flown in. All of which led, the morning after my gaffe in the restaurant, to an encounter that left me feeling even more like some fog-shrouded, incorrigibly backwoods Elderberry Finn.

The latter image seems especially apt now, looking back on the experience, because the Frenchman's office was barely a hundred yards from the Seine. And the morning was in fact cloaked in a chill fog when I stood nervously on the street, double-checking the address, before pressing the bell. A plump, gray-haired woman suddenly materialized at my side as I stood there, her shopping basket stuffed with fresh vegetables, and asked if she could help. Warmed with gratitude, I followed her up the dimly lit steps to an inconspicuous little doorway on the first floor. Smiling and nodding, she assured me that it was indeed Monsieur Affre's office, then climbed on and vanished up the narrow stair.

The figure that answered my hesitant knock was as unpretentious, as unstereotypically Parisian, as the humble setting. A short, middle-aged man in wire-rim glasses and a ratty brown sweater, he greeted me politely and cleared what little space he could in a room small enough we sat getting acquainted in a pair of chairs squeezed so close together our knees occasionally brushed. I relaxed a bit when it became apparent his English was both fluent and informal, and we soon found ourselves chatting comfortably about the arcane world of fly-fishing. I relaxed even more when he muttered his quiet approval of the half-dozen hand-tied flies I'd brought along. Still, though he'd been hospitable from the beginning, I was stunned when he abruptly stood up and casually invited me to lunch at his home a few doors up the street.

The night before, in our brief phone contact, I'd been promised fifteen or twenty minutes out of his workday. I suddenly found myself seated instead in another upstairs room that was slightly larger but no less intimate than his office—the kitchen of a snug apartment bright with flowers and ceramic art. Thoroughly charmed, I reveled in the delicious *salade composée* his wife had fixed for us, the raindrops softly pattering on the kitchen window, the free-flowing conversation, on a rich variety of topics, as their two school-age children, also home for lunch, ate from plates of pasta and occasionally joined in.

I had begun my trip hoping to touch the soul of provincial France, a place where life, at least in memory, moved to the gentler village rhythms of my youth. And against all expectation, I had found something wondrously close to it a few hundred yards from the *Champs Elysée*. The Affres had a kindness that felt completely instinctive, without pomp or pretense, flowing quietly on with the seeming ease of breathing in spaces so diminutive a supersized world wouldn't notice them at all.

And then something happened that culminated with a coincidence I still find almost too unlikely to believe. Having lost all track of time in the intoxicating idyll, I glanced down at my watch and rose apologetically from the table, embarrassed by the sudden realization I'd kept my genial host for over an hour from the afternoon work he'd mentioned the night before that he needed to do. Shaking his head dismissively, he insisted it wasn't a problem, then rose too and led me up the hallway stair to yet another cramped and cluttered space below the building's roof, this one stuffed from floor to rafters with a stunning assemblage of ancient rods, lures, creels, and other dusty artifacts from a lifetime spent fishing countless waters around the globe. Rummaging through a pile on his desk, he came up with a volume listing the five hundred best in France, which he nonchalantly handed me as a gift. Taken aback, I mumbled a sincere thanks—told him the book would be especially useful when I revisited a part of Languedoc whose trout streams had enchanted me ten years earlier, on a two-month sabbatical stay with my wife. "Where in Languedoc were you?" he asked, looking mildly interested. "A little village called Montpeyroux, north of Montpellier," I replied.

"*Montpeyroux!*?" he cried out, surprise flooding his face. The village had fewer than eight hundred residents. For a Parisian to know of it, as he obviously did, was the equivalent of a New Yorker knowing some remote hamlet in South Carolina or Maine. "Montpeyroux," he repeated, shaking his head. One of his best friends had once lived there, he said, and in another bizarre coincidence, a documentary film partly set in the vineyards on its outskirts had recently hit Paris with the critical force of a *succès de scandale*.

I absolutely had to see it, he went on, given what I'd told him at lunch about my trip objectives and the fact I'd once been a temporary resident of the tiny village. Digging into another heaping mound of books and articles, he came up with a recent review of the film he had xeroxed from *The New York Times*. In the next couple of minutes, as he switched his computer on and downloaded a digital fishing video he'd made recently, I hastily scanned the review's first few paragraphs:

"It's not often that French movie circles and French wine circles are buzzing about the same thing," it began, *"but 'Mondovino,' Jonathan*

Nossiter's documentary about the globalization of wine, has movie critics here reaching for superlatives and some wine experts lobbing expletives, while audiences have turned the movie into a surprise hit....*

"More than a wine documentary," the piece continued, in a passage that both reinforced my trip hopes and filled me with foreboding, "'Mondovino' is a passionate defense of the individuality of small wine producers in a more standardized world...."

For the next fifteen minutes, as I watched Pierre's own beautifully crafted video on Atlantic salmon fishing in Russia, my mind remained torn between the pulse-stirring river scenes in front of me and the *Times* reviewer's unsettling account of *"an invasion from abroad"*... *"a fight between the Resistance and the collaborators"*... *"an off-the-record comment in which a chauffeur-driven Bordeaux agent for such corporate wine empires as Robert Mondavi and Mouton-Rothschild called Languedoc residents who had fought to prevent his client (Mondavi) from setting up shop in France 'hicks'."*

When the video ended, I expressed my genuine appreciation of its quality, thanking him once more for the unforgettable hospitality he and his wife had shown me. But the disquieting review's impact must have been obvious. A quizzical smile on his lips, he asked me what I'd thought of it. Still grappling with the rush of events, I mumbled a half-coherent answer, then listened with an even deeper sense of foreboding as he added his own somber comments on the imperiled state of French rural culture, a grim sketch that sounded depressingly similar to my own past laments for the faded villages of my youth.

Our meeting might have ended there, but the mercurial Frenchman wasn't quite done. Walking me back down the creaking staircase to the street, he led me several hundred yards farther on a brisk three-block walk to the nearest kiosk for a copy of the weekly *Pariscope* to see if the film was still playing. And finding that it was, he shepherded me two more blocks down narrow, intersecting streets to where he could point my way to the theatre door.

We bid a quick *au revoir* at that point and he was gone, as indelible a presence in the weeks that followed as the documentary I spent the next two hours raptly watching, my emotions riding a turbulent course from inspiration through anger, sadness, and dismay. But along with a visceral rage at the corporate invaders' soulless contempt for centuries of rural tradition, I felt an equally intense pride that the little Languedoc villages they indifferently dismissed as peasant hicksvilles had stood valiantly up to them, as the region's Résistance *Maquis* had battled the Nazis sixty years before. A central part of the film had focused on one of those tiny outposts, Aniane, a place I remembered vividly. Less than ten miles from Montpeyroux, Jane and I had visited it often during our sabbatical stay and been treated warmly. Exiting the theatre, I wondered what welcome awaited me now, a probing American, when I walked its medieval streets a few days hence.

The morning mist had turned into an evening rain, but I decided to walk the mile or so back along the Seine to the hotel regardless, stopping only at an Internet café to send a brief email home to my absent wife in the States. The haunting film and the familial warmth of the Affres had conspired to drop me into that melancholy funk I've known only in cities, even one as magical as Paris at dusk. But as I trudged on, reflecting on the improbable events that had marked my first twenty-four hours in the country, my spirits gradually began to lift. The gallant resistance of those tiny Languedoc villages to the corporate moneymen had something to do with it, however bleak their future, as did the loveliness of the wet, streetlit walk along the Seine. But it was the memory of my restaurant gaffe the night before that lingered—that and the further recollections it triggered of similar "hicksville" gaucheries I had committed in the past. The thought had never occurred to me before, but what I slowly came to realize, reliving them, was that nearly all had been blessings in disguise—had opened doors I'd never otherwise have entered—and that the tolerant way the French, even the Parisian French, responded to them felt a lot like the lost America of my youth.

One incident in particular flooded back with acute clarity, for it had happened at that most self-conscious of ages, sixteen. It was a Thursday night, in the depths of winter. In proud possession of the driver's license I'd somehow managed to gain a few weeks earlier, I set off with my best friend after basketball practice to hunt jackrabbits in the sandhills north of town. Like the weekend road-hunting of which it was an especially crazed, nighttime variant, this adventure too was blatantly illegal, but if you grew up on the prairie in the 1950's you won't be surprised it was one of the things that passed back then as fun. And in any case the sport, if it can be called that, was almost as hazardous to the hunter as to the rabbits, given our bone-jarring practice of firing through the dim beam of a hand-held spotlight from a moving vehicle as it bounced over the gopher-holed and wheel-rutted plains.

The few rabbits we managed to kill were sold as food to mink farms—another part of my benighted youth, but that's a different story—and in this instance my friend Jim and I had shot three or four. The vehicle was my father's, an old wood-paneled station wagon that met its own demise a few months later when the engine burned out for lack of oil. (This further example of the family gene for macho-shriveling humiliation is one more story best left untold.) In any case, the problem on this night was not the old beater's engine but its tail lights, or rather their absence, since a single bulb burning faintly above the rattling exhaust pipe was the only rear illumination it had. The grizzled "rabbitman," as we called him, lived on the far edge of the village just beyond the streetlights, his house recessed at the end of a long, chicken-coop-bordered driveway barely wide enough for a car to pass through. Driving in was no problem. It was the return that became one of those mortifying teenage experiences you never forget.

Our half-dollar of blood money stuffed in our jeans, Jim tried to navigate me back down that dark reverse course out to the street, but I'd backed only a few feet before a loud, bumper-rattling thunk stopped us with jolting abruptness. Climbing out in confusion, we blamed each other for the screwup, then spent the next five minutes restacking the chunks of elm I'd knocked off the woodpile near the rabbitman's coop of clucking hens. Climbing back into the old Ford, we resumed our myopic descent toward the street.

We'd moved maybe another fifteen or twenty feet when a louder reverberation shook the vehicle—a metallic clank followed immediately by a jetting gush of water so torrential we sat stunned for what felt like an eternity watching the windshield disappear in rivers of rain. Eventually we climbed numbly out again, the water already rising above the soles of our hunting boots. This time I had backed into a fire hydrant, snapping it off at the ground like a toppled red gnome.

If Jim Brand alone had remained privy to this Everest of humiliations, I probably would not be writing about it now, however abashed I remained for weeks afterward. But even back then Silver Creek, Nebraska, contained fewer than five hundred people. A single hydrant served the entire west half of the village, which is where the city fathers decades earlier had unfortunately chosen to build the school. As a result of what I'd accidentally done, all twelve grades had to be closed the following morning. Which gave me even more time, cloistered in my upstairs bedroom, to contemplate the broader implications of the deed.

Somehow I got through that afternoon's torturous round of classes and the blitzkrieg of jibes that filled the hallways. I even survived without too many permanent scars to my psyche the reception from the rest of the town that evening, when I dribbled miserably out of the locker room onto the basketball court leading my team into our bandbox gym. (Our coach, who loved a good joke, had ceremoniously named me the game captain for the only time that year.) But it was not until that rainy evening in Paris, walking along the Seine, that I felt something approaching gratitude for the ironic gift such experiences had given me—a lasting inoculation against the withering fear of embarrassment and subsequent paralysis that can shrink one's world of experience to a cramped safe house devoid of risk. At the cost of an admittedly painful prick to my ego, I'd been given a kind of carte blanche to snatch the flotsam that so often bizarrely seemed to follow in its wake.

In hindsight, the raucous teasing I'd received on that longest twenty-four hours of my life was mostly good-natured, even when administered by my needling classmates, a kid-glove treatment that no doubt reflected their own collective sense of liberation. (None of them would have acknowledged it to me, but they all knew they'd lucked into a half day of freedom thanks to my bonehead play.) When I finally regained my bearings, the experience had helped transform me from the most faint-hearted of underclassmen to a kid capable, at least occasionally, of looking a senior in the eye when we passed in the hall.

More often than not in my life, such maladroit acts had ended with a similar serendipity. My first year out of college, a wide-eyed *naif* from a straightlaced little prairie church school suddenly awash in southern California's sexy allure, I had impulsively bought a surfboard, tried to ride a wave totally oblivious of the fact I'd somehow turned the alien thing upside down beneath me, and found a day-long mentor when I gurgled up out of the inevitable wipeout and saw a bronze-skinned native laughing hysterically on the beach. In my later career as a college professor, two of my favorite classes had grown out of similar ice-breaking travesties—the first when I'd breezily embarked on a lecture unaware that my fly was open and the other a chalkboard fiasco when a protruding screw, having ripped out the seat of my pants, forced a backwards retreat to my office, a red-faced return in a jogging suit, and the only standing ovation I've ever received. As I said, the gene is familial. Among my father's countless modeling examples, I'll add only that he once ran out of gas in a funeral procession; complained to his ten-year-old grandson about the "ridiculously tough crust" of a pizza only to be told he'd just eaten a piece of cheese-covered cardboard; and well into his seventies, hooked the hat off the head of Nebraska's senior Senator with a bass lure he'd tried to cast into a windswept lake.

I don't know if my father reached the end of his life ever having had the same epiphany I had in Paris. And it may be that *epiphany* is too grandiose a word for the moment of awareness I've just described. But you think of a lot of things, walking through the rain at night along a river. And that night on the left bank of the Seine, one of those things was this: there was a time in the United States, before we discovered road rage and a we'll-kick-your-ass foreign policy and the private ownership of assault weapons as every red-blooded patriot's divine right, when things felt a lot quieter, a lot less edgy and defensive. And despite the concerns *Mondovino* had stirred in me, my first few hours in the country had reinforced my belief that such old-world civilities were still deeply valued in France. A polite "*Bonjour*" or "*Excusez-moi*" was still the coinage of the realm, capable of the timeless alchemy it had always worked, and that fact felt both uniquely French and reassuringly familiar. Felt the way it had felt decades earlier watching my father knock on a farmhouse door to ask if we could hunt the back forty or fish the reedy pond behind the barnyard, maybe stop back an hour or two later to leave a few bullheads or a pheasant if we'd had any luck.

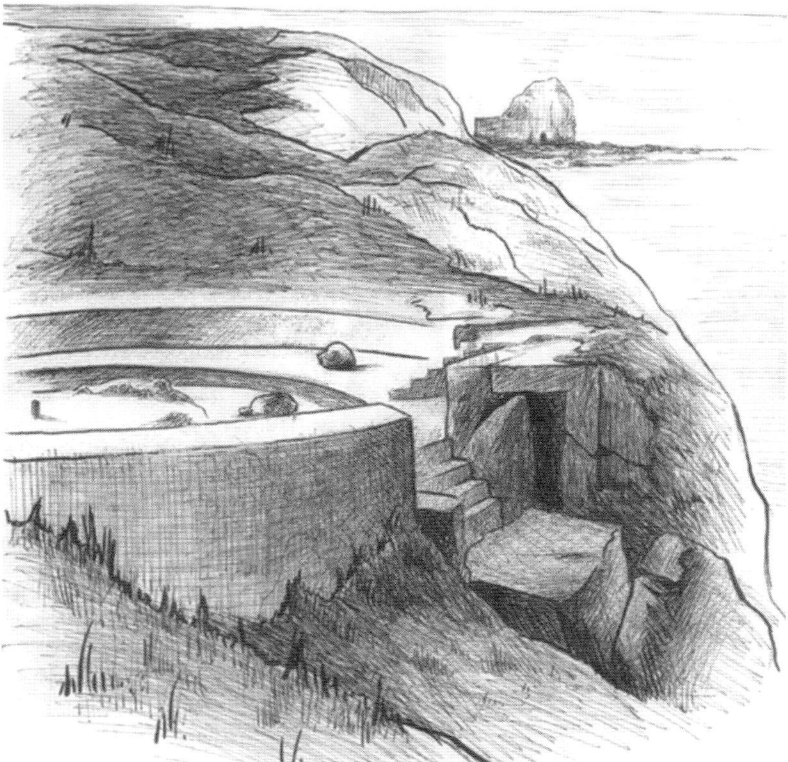

Chapter 3
Back In Time

You leave the dirt path and step over a single strand of barbed wire, disregarding the "*Attention!*" sign as many others have obviously done before you, then creep on toward the cliff face and drop cautiously to your knees. A hundred yards below is the beach, pounded by the sea, and you briefly close your eyes against the sudden wash of acrophobia. You lie now on your stomach, your right hand anchored inside the concrete throat of a German bunker. When at last you turn and peer into its cavernous depths, the air of menace sweeps you back most of a lifetime to a day it remains impossible to comprehend.

I had visited Pointe du Hoc in the mid-1990's, on the same afternoon I walked the immaculate rows of white crosses in the Army cemetery a few kilometers distant. It is possible, if only barely, to express the mix of sorrow, pride, and boundless gratitude an American feels at the military gravesite. I don't believe that words, or even such a graphic film as *Saving Private Ryan*, can begin to capture one's incredulity staring down off that cliff edge and imagining the team of Army Rangers that captured it on that momentous day sixty years ago.

I'd lain a long time beside that empty bunker, trying to get my mind around their sacrifice. Immediately behind me the earth remained a moonscape of bomb craters and grotesquely twisted metal, the expanse of beach below only a scant few miles from where William the Conqueror had launched his own Channel-crossing invasion nearly a millennium before. Over the years, I'd become deeply ambivalent about patriotism, increasingly repelled by the supercilious lapel pins and jingoistic flag-waving that had taken on a knee-jerk reflexiveness in much of my homeland. But in those minutes of prone silence above Omaha Beach, I had felt only reverence for America's bedrock virtues. Rising, I picked my way back across the cratered earth much as one moves after awakening from some particularly haunting dream.

A second experience, two years later, had reinforced my decision to make Normandy the first of my trip destinations after leaving Paris in the rented car. Traveling alone then as well, I'd stopped one night in another of the small hotel-restaurants—this one happened to be in Burgundy—that so often brought strangers together in the kind of quiet social intimacy unknown in the corporate chain lodgings which had largely replaced them decades earlier in the United States. An old man and his wife were sitting across from me, two younger men slightly farther off at a table in the corner, and for over an hour the room was silent except for the murmur of their separate conversations and our mutual savoring of the food. I had finished my dessert and was about to leave when the old man spoke a few words to me. A mutual exchange of travelers' information followed, soon joined by the pair of younger Frenchmen. Both of them were clearly as interested as I was when the scattered conversation eventually touched on World War II and I mentioned how moved I'd been by those endless rows of manicured graves—by the gaping maws of bunkers still embedded above the beach at Pointe du Hoc. Nodding somberly, the old man cleared his throat and added softly that in his Maquis unit, down in Languedoc, nearly half the men had died.

I can't attest to the words' truth, only that they struck me as neither a boast nor a defensive whitewash of France's shameful Vichy collaboration, and that what appeared to stir him most was simply the fact I was an attentive American, which pleased him enough he asked the waiter to bring a shot of Armagnac to my table when he ordered his own. When the drinks arrived, he raised his glass to me, and with his other hand mimed the lifting of a hat in tribute. "*Chapeau, monsieur,*" he said, bowing stiffly. "*Chapeau.*"

The gesture would have humbled me had I never seen the killing fields where so many men of his generation had perished. Having seen them, I felt both gratitude and a profound unworthiness. I'd done absolutely nothing to deserve the homage, and remained in awe of those who had. But I was an American. The old man clearly came from a time when that fact alone merited a tip of the cap if you were French.

More recent events, unfortunately, had driven a wedge between our two countries which gave that heartwarming experience the faded feel of a scrapbook memory. I arrived in the village of Arromanches-les-Bains, ground zero for the D-Day invasion, hoping at least a little of the old bonhomie remained. But if it didn't, I hoped to learn that too. The immediate problem was how to do so. Would I find anyone willing to speak at length, let alone in depth, with an American stranger in a town whose only current invasions were the tens of thousands of tourists who descended on it each year?

But how many of them showed up in February, I tried to buck up my resolve, laboring to turn the whipping onshore wind and sub-freezing temperatures into some kind of advantage as I descended the hill into the little town at dusk. My spirits rose a few degrees at its first impression. The place showed little outward sign of change since my previous visit a decade earlier. If anything, the absence of tourists made it feel even more as if I'd stepped back into the past. Tidy winter-shuttered houses. A half dozen small hotels. A few other modest, nondescript little businesses clustered on the single commercial street just above the beach. It was like imagining Gettysburg or the Alamo without the encroaching ring of Super Eights and Pizza Huts. My relief was palpable as I drove on.

The hotel Jane and I had stayed in previously was closed for the winter, and repeated knocking at the weathered door of a second failed to roust anyone out despite a sign declaring it open, just up the street. Stymied, I drove back up the hill and stopped at a third on the edge of town, a crowing red rooster painted on a gatepost by the road. The owner sat bent over his account book when I entered, his glasses perched at the tip of his long Gallic nose. "*Oui, monsieur?*" he said, peering at me impassively over the rims, not uncordial but clearly occupied with his work.

"*Pardon, monsieur,*" I responded uncertainly. "*Avez-vous une chambre libre pour ce soir?*" The question felt slightly ridiculous given the deserted look of the village and the absence of any vehicle but my own in the parking lot. Still, it felt good to fall back into the old protocols on this, my first night in the campagne—felt as if I'd drifted back in time, and was getting back in time with it, the small-town rhythm of my youth. *Oui*, the owner assured me nonchalantly, he did indeed have a room. The *prix* was fifty-five euros. Turning slightly in his chair, he nodded toward a discreet sign with the posted rates taped on the office wall.

It was only a euro less per night than I had paid for my room in Paris, and the fact momentarily disconcerted me. Even so, if the dollar hadn't recently taken yet another plunge down the foreign exchange sinkhole I probably wouldn't have hesitated—let my mind run on to another small inn I thought I'd glimpsed just up the road. But as I stood there, briefly weighing the options, the balding hotelier shrugged and spoke again, this time in English. "So how much you wish to pay?" he asked, faintly smiling. "Forty euros? The room is good." I told him I was sure it was and said yes to his offer at once without checking, more than a little shame-faced at the reduction. The moment of budget-conscious hesitation felt even pettier when I returned from the car with my luggage. The third-floor *chambre* proved to be as fine as he'd promised, complete with lace curtains, a large window overlooking a snow-dusted garden, and an ancient toilet it took me several minutes to learn how to flush.

It was the kind of quirky, beguiling experience that had drawn me back to France. The next morning, after spending several more head-scratching minutes decoding the shower, I descended the footworn stair filled with fresh resolve.

The phlegmatic owner was back at his post, and after sincerely thanking him again for his hospitality, I briefly explained what had brought me to Arromanches. He nodded thoughtfully as he listened, took several moments to consider, then scrawled two names on a slip of paper and handed it to me. "*M. Duchez*," read the first. The second, "*M. Marot*." "They are old men now," he said, "but they were here during *l'invasion*. Perhaps they will speak to you. I do not know. *Bonne chance*."

I drove back down into the village and parked beside the invasion museum, its snow-sprinkled lot empty and the gate open with no attendant or fee. The hotel owner hadn't said where either of the two old men lived, only that they remained local residents, and I set off uncertainly up the deserted streets hoping to meet someone who might know. The wind had diminished but the temperature still hung at minus-seven Celsius—barely twenty degrees above zero. At eight-thirty in the morning, the village was shut up like a fist.

I had seen no one in several minutes of fruitless searching when I met a bundled and shawled woman walking her dog. Yes, she nodded, she knew both men. Monsieur Duchez and his wife, in fact, lived just up the street from where we stood. Pointing, she turned abruptly on her heel and led me and the leashed dog a hundred yards back in the direction they had just traveled, stopping in front of a small shuttered house with no door that I could see. A chest-high fence shielded a tiny garden. Pausing only to unlatch the gate, the woman walked in, waving at someone I could dimly make out through a gleaming windowpane.

The old man who appeared at the house's rear door a minute later was slightly stooped and wearing carpet slippers, but his big-boned frame was robust beneath a round open face. He greeted the woman warmly, and when she told him *monsieur* had been searching for his residence, he turned to me and nodded, his craggy eyebrows lifting in bewilderment. I thanked the woman for her help as she turned to leave, the dog straining at its leash ahead of her, then followed the old man into his dining room, where he invited me to sit down at a cherrywood table polished to a high sheen. The room was small but tastefully decorated. In the best French I could muster, I told him why I had come.

Over the next half-hour, while the two of us sat talking, his shyly smiling wife made several brief appearances as she moved through her morning routine of domestic duties, but there was otherwise no sound but our quiet flow of words in the tidy house. He was seven on the day of the great *bombardement*, the old Frenchman told me—a little boy who watched the opening salvos through the upstairs window of the house next door, holding his ears. Shortly afterward the family had taken refuge in the cellar. He could still hear the whistle of the shells passing over, he said—their explosions shaking the earth just outside the village. The German soldiers had run past shouting and giving orders in the streets.

He had much more to say, about events then and now, but it soon became depressingly clear this first interview of the trip was destined to serve mostly as a rude wake-up call to the formidable obstacles I faced if my objectives were to be realized. For as intently as I listened, I couldn't understand more than occasional snatches of his French. I left the house far more frustrated than enlightened, though the gracious old couple had done everything they could to help.

An hour later I stood staring up at the home of M. and Mme. Marot. The names were clearly lettered on the curbside mailbox. So also, unnervingly, was the much larger "*Attention aux Chiens!*" sign on the locked metal gate. The house was on the edge of the village, perched atop a slope, behind a thigh-high stone wall that shielded it from the street. The gatepost had no bell or buzzer—no way at all that I could see, short of shouting, to determine if anyone was at home. After standing on the pavement for some time pondering the options, I finally decided it would do little good to return later in the day since a solution to the dilemma wasn't likely to be any more apparent then. Suppressing the "Beware of Dogs" sign, I hopped over the wall on a brazen impulse and climbed up the slope to the front door.

The dogs sounded as ferocious as advertised. Fortunately, they were only slightly bigger than a pair of Chihuahuas, and their teeth snapped at me from behind a pane of glass. When several knocks still brought no sign of their owners, I returned to the street even more frustrated than I'd been leaving the Duchez' home. If my search for the soul of provincial France rested on the early omens, they could hardly have been worse.

And then I caught a stroke of blind, improbably good luck. I had trudged most of the short distance back to where I'd parked my car, when the murmur of a vehicle creeping slowly over wet pavement whispered behind me, and I turned to see a small sedan pull up at the Marots' gate. Five minutes later I sat at another gleaming table, this time in the company of a small, neatly groomed Frenchman and his loquacious wife.

Monsieur Marot was as thin and sharply defined as his clipped gray mustache, the pristine interior of the house another testament to quiet good taste. And as if the fates had somehow singled me out for a prolonged run of good fortune, I could understand most of the French both of them spoke. For the next hour, the three of us sat talking about the momentous events the couple had witnessed over sixty years earlier, as well as the current state of the world. He was thirteen at the time of "*la grande invasion,*" the old man began softly in answer to my opening question, living in the next village a few kilometers to the east. The Germans had occupied it for four years but they were always "*correct*" with the citizens. Life went on, things were "*normales,*" though there were "*beaucoup de restrictions*" on what they could eat and drink. But even this, his wife interjected, was far less troublesome than in the cities. In the country, with all the farmers, they were "*moins privés que les villes*"—much less deprived.

Were their houses searched by the Germans, I asked. "*Oui,*" they nodded, often, and by the British and Americans as well, later on. The two of them shared a laugh about a Czech "secret agent" everyone in the town knew was feeding the Germans information because he spoke such bad French. Recounting the story, they were kind enough not to mention my own glaring mispronunciations, and I moved gratefully on.

What was the invasion like, I asked.

The night before, Monsieur Marot responded, there was "*une certaine agitation*" among the Germans, but no one in the village knew anything. The next morning the sky suddenly turned "*rouge*," he added somberly, filled with sights and sounds he would never forget. With the rest of his family, he ran for a sunken shelter in the garden. The "*deluge de feu*," or firestorm, went on for several hours. Several residents of the town were killed, and by midafternoon people were desperate to flee but the Germans forced them to return to the shelters. When at last it was over and the English took the town, they cried out in joy.

We had reached a point where the questions I felt compelled to ask them got a lot dicier, and I paused, clearing my throat, before carrying on. What were their feelings now, I asked, more than a half-century later, toward the countries that had launched the massive invasion, which in the cruel inevitability of war had both liberated their homeland and left thousands of French citizens dead in its wake.

We get along with them well to this day, the old man said, smiling. One of his closest friends was a British soldier who had said "Good day" to his grandmother during the liberation. He was ninety-three now and lived in Liverpool, yet they corresponded often. During the coming summer, he planned to return for a visit to Arromanches.

And what of America today, I continued, even more hesitantly. Our two countries no longer seemed able to get along nearly as well.

A long pause followed, the old couple looking at each other in silence, deciding who would respond.

It doesn't affect us directly, Madame Marot finally answered. Governments disagree. They always have. We have no reason to see things any differently than before.

A lot of people over here still think of "*ce rêve américain*," her husband added, leaning toward me in his chair, so they remain sympathetic. Many young people are still going to follow it, "*ce rêve américain*." He repeated the phrase in French, peering into my eyes—*this American dream*.

What do you think of President Bush, I risked.

The Americans must be content if they re-elected him, the old man answered tentatively, his wife nodding in agreement. Again they glanced silently at each other, deferring to whoever felt inclined to say more. The Iraq war was a war of liberation, Madame Marot murmured, like Tunisia or Algeria. Or it might be. France was too far away for them to draw any firm conclusions—to know what was happening for sure. (Two hours earlier, in one of the few responses I'd understood clearly, I had been told the same thing by Monsieur Duchez.)

As the conversation wound down I took a last look around the snug, beautifully appointed room and silently pondered what the morning's experiences had revealed. The most obvious inference was that the French of Arromanches, at least the village's oldest generation, appeared to have retained their good will toward America and Americans, even to the point of withholding judgment on a government the several Parisiens I'd spoken to had denounced in words close to contempt. The second impression was more figurative but felt more certain. In a pointed irony far too few of my Frog-bashing countrymen had had my good luck to discover, French homes mirrored the French personality—taut, battened-down exteriors that disguised the quiet warmth one found inside.

A few minutes later, tamping down the breezy familiarity that comes so easily to a twenty-first-century middle-American but had once, at least on the Plains, been far rarer, I thanked the couple genuinely and rose to leave. But like Pierre Affre in Paris, my aged host had other ideas. He needed the exercise and would walk down into the village with me, he said, pulling on a wool coat and a blue beret. Startled but pleased, I didn't tell him that my car was parked less than fifty yards away, and remained mute as we trooped slowly past it. The beachfront was only another few hundred yards farther on, but our pace was delayed less by the distance and the old man's bad hip than by his several stops to greet other locals. It too had an old-world feel, the presence of townspeople out on the streets, walking. Occasionally I spoke a deferential word or two but for the most part simply stood silently and watched, privy for a few absorbed moments to the gentle undercurrents of this tiny town whose five hundred residents had somehow managed to retain their rural character on a site hordes of foreigners invaded every year. Eventually we met the middle-aged laborer who had pointed my way up the hill to the Marot house two hours earlier, both of them chuckling over my dapper companion's introductory comment that their shared first name, Marcel, was "the most distinguished name in France"—and then a few steps farther on, Monsieur Duchez, returning from the *boulangerie*. For the next several minutes, the two old men who had witnessed one of the most violent cataclysms in human history stood quietly chatting as I watched and listened, one cradling a *baguette* in his still sturdy arm, the other nodding and smiling under his beret.

The image remained with me an hour later as my car rolled to a stop in the nearly empty parking lot at Pointe du Hoc. In the late afternoon quiet, the gently rolling farmland beyond the footpath was serene, almost eerily pastoral. A small tractor pulling a manure spreader was creeping over a patch of ground in the distance. Walking the quarter-mile to the cliff's edge, I watched it turn and slowly retrace its course. The diminutive size of both—machine and field—appeared as natural here as they'd have felt jarringly anachronistic back home.

I paused for a moment listening to the tractor's throaty pull, as familiar as the vividly remembered chug and bright red hue of a 50's Farmall, then walked on to the battlefield. Its moonscape craters and concrete gun emplacements sustained the feeling of a time warp as I crested a rise and approached the cliff.

The sagging strand of barbed wire was gone, replaced by a head-high mesh fence and a new sign warning *"Danger! N'entrez pas. Éboulement de falaises!"* I had to check my pocket dictionary to learn that *"éboulement"* meant collapse or landslide, but the meaning was clear without it. There would be no more peering over the *falaise* edge, clutching the bunker and trying to fathom the courage that had led 225 American soldiers to acts of such immeasurable bravery only ninety of them had survived. The rest had died within yards of where I stood, fighting to liberate a country with one of the bloodiest histories in Europe. I thought of the savage religious wars of the fifteenth and sixteenth centuries. Of Robespierre and The Terror. Of France's long and brutal period of colonization—its own past adventurism in Iran and Iraq.

I stared again at the bucolic scene just beyond the last tangle of rusted metal, untouched by time. The little tractor was still moving across the near horizon, its faint growl barely audible over the tides gnawing at the beach below.

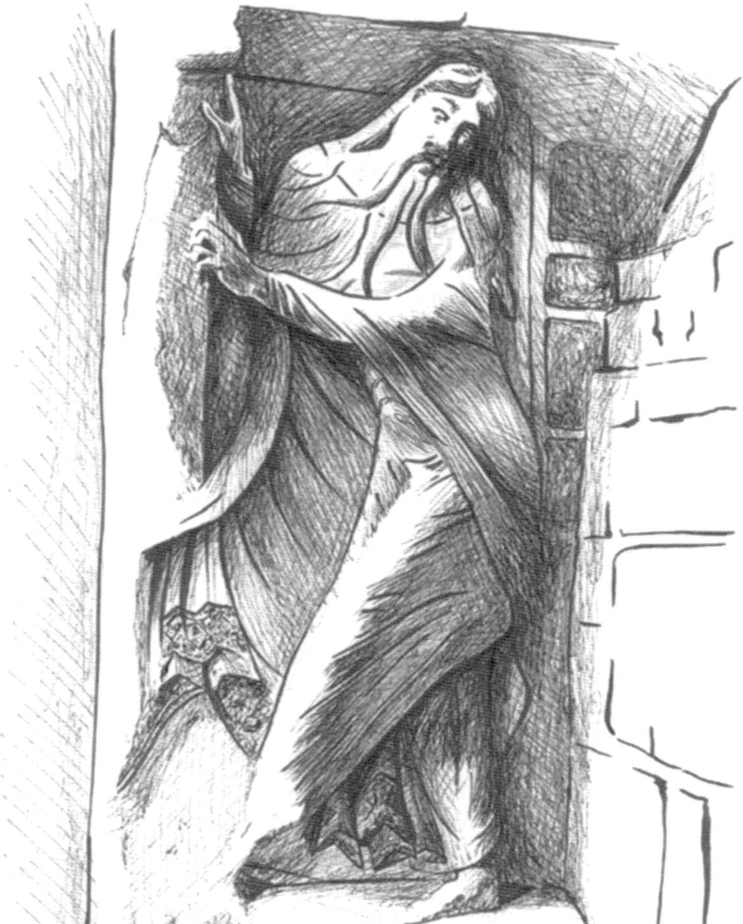

Chapter 4
Isaiah

To grow up on the Plains in the middle of the last century left a lot of time to kill for those of us not shackled, as most farmers were, to a work day of dawn to dark. In my family, when we weren't hunting or fishing, most of that time was devoted to church and to sports, though to an outsider's eye the distinction would probably have appeared redundant. The countless football, basketball, and baseball games we avidly played, watched, and listened to on the radio had much the same hold on our lives as the Holy Trinity we publicly worshipped every Sunday at the Methodist Church.

The latter devotion had faded long before my flight to France, but the blood-deep love of sports remained. I had chosen as my next trip destination the small town of Souillac, at the edge of the Dordogne, in nostalgic memory of a day seven years earlier when the two most deeply resonant chords from my youth had once again throbbed as one. On that midsummer afternoon, four friends in tow, my wife and I had returned to the town's monastic abbey to view a bas-relief of the prophet Isaiah, one of the uncelebrated jewels of medieval sculpture. It happened also to be the day France played Brazil in the climactic game of the 1998 World Cup of soccer, or "football," as the planet's most popular sport is known outside the United States. Jane and I had made our initial pilgrimage to the abbey church on a chilly March day several years earlier, aware only of the Isaiah's quiet reputation among medievalists as a Romanesque masterpiece. Road-weary and stiff after a four-hour drive from Languedoc, we'd trooped distractedly into the sanctuary and found ourselves instantly, utterly transported. The sculpture's evocation of fluid grace and cool austerity was unlike anything either of us had ever seen.

I lingered even longer in the church on that second, midsummer visit, finally drifting away to a brasserie a few blocks up the street only because I had an equally absorbing interest in *La Coupe du Monde*. Though the game would be played in Paris, the French were such heavy underdogs even their own fans didn't think they could win against the soccer titans from South America. Adding to the mystique of the Brazilians' multiple world titles was the style of *futbol* they played—wondrously fluid, improvisational, quick-striking—and the fact that their most renowned players were known by a single, heart-stirringly poetic name. *Pelé, Socrates, Falcao, Ronaldo*. The last was the current team's resident super-talent, and the championship match promised to be a David/Goliath clash of epic proportions. Still dazzled by the Isaiah's sublime power, I felt on that July afternoon as if I'd been doubly blessed by the gods.

The intensity of that remembered experience, strong enough to have drawn me back a third time to the remote little town in the French interior, is difficult to communicate. But perhaps a bit more background on the culture and family I grew up in will help.

I'll begin with a frank admission. From the vantage point of anyone who hasn't grown up there, it's doubtful there's ever been such a thing as "normal life" in Nebraska. If it ever existed, for the last half century it's ground to a dead stop every football Saturday in even the most isolated villages throughout the state. And by "state," I refer not merely to the geographical entity but to the mental condition that afflicts tens of thousands of people whose roots are there, wherever we now might live.

My younger brother Doug, to cite only the most proximate example, is a cardiovascular surgeon in Madison, Wisconsin who has been ranked by several objective criteria as one of the most skilled heart specialists in the state. Yet for over three decades this pillar of medical professionalism has kept a plastic Cornhusker helmet above the scrubs in his locker, the last thing he looks at before "putting on his game face" (as he puts it) and entering the operating room. I trust it won't expose him to threats of malpractice if I add that a few years back, an hour before the Cornhuskers took the field in the Orange Bowl to play for a national championship against Miami, he was so wired with pre-game anxiety he walked down to the lake behind his house and threw up on the shore.

It's an affliction maybe only a Cubs or Red Sox fan will recognize, though in the latter case it may have diminished slightly with their recent World Series victory. And since Nebraska did finally beat Miami in that bowl game after a decade of bitter failures, I'm reasonably certain my brother's stomach has remained more or less intact ever since. But if the sports bug has bitten you deep, you know one thing with total conviction. You're *always* vulnerable. My own life serves as another case in point—or more accurately, two cases, since my similar devotion to Husker football was outstripped in my youth by a fervor for the Brooklyn Dodgers that approached a self-flagellating medieval saint's.

The comparison may seem ludicrous but feels accurate to me now for three reasons. First, throughout my childhood in the late 40's and early 50's, the Dodgers *always* lost when it counted most, scoring years of pain on my anguished soul. Second, not long after they finally managed to win a World Series, the team abruptly fled Brooklyn for Los Angeles, a shameless money-grab that left me feeling both betrayed and anchorless, as cursed by an inscrutable fate as Job. It was the third influence, though, flowing subliminally on for decades after my Dodger loyalty had withered, that traced an unbroken course down to that remote French church and its statue of Isaiah: a revered athlete who came to have the same lasting purchase on my emotions the Old Testament prophet clearly had for the anonymous medieval artist who carved his spirit out of stone.

To say that I was spiritually transported by the diamond wizardry of Sandy Koufax would be an exaggeration, but not by much. He'd become my boyhood hero almost from the moment I first read about him as a flame-throwing but incorrigibly wild Dodger "bonus baby" who sat unused on the Brooklyn bench through several seasons in the mid-1950's. Then, miraculously, as if calmed by the beatific climes of Los Angeles, the scattergun wildness that had plagued him for years was suddenly harnessed—the wondrous but fragile left arm freed to exploits so extraordinary it was as if one of his scorching fastballs had burned into my soul. One particularly telling personal experience from that magical run remains undimmed in my mind's eye to this day.

The incident would no doubt long since have faded from memory if I'd been alone, in my upstairs bedroom, as I usually was on those sweltering summer evenings, hanging breathlessly on every pitch as the unhittable Sandy etched yet another mound gem in the record books. But I wasn't. I was sitting in my car with a girl on a secluded sandhill not far from where Jim Brand and I had shot those fateful jackrabbits two years earlier. And where the opposite sex was concerned, I remained as green and feckless as I'd been back then—so painfully shy and inexperienced I'd had my first kiss at the junior-senior prom, barely a month before. On this moonlit night, in short, I found myself on perhaps the third or fourth actual date of my life, the first (and soon to be last) with an attractive blonde named Janet Martin. I liked her. She seemed to like me, or at least so I tremblingly inferred from the fact she'd said nothing when, en route home from a movie, I'd abruptly turned the car off the highway into those windswept reaches of switchgrass and sand.

Did I have "parking" in mind? Emphatically. Though at that stage of my sexual experience, "first base' would have been the furthest I could possibly have dreamed. What astonishes me now, in retrospect—continues to register as some weird fusion of physical and ascetic devotion—is that the stirrings in my loins were fully matched by those in my brain, which kept whispering that it was eleven o'clock at night, *nine o'clock out in Los Angeles*, and Sandy was on the hill. Lying on my upstairs bed on several such cloudless nights earlier in the summer, I'd been able to pick up Vin Scully's game broadcasts on my transistor radio, fading in and out like threads of gossamer over the deserts and mountains stretching half a continent between. But I'd been alone then. Free to spend hours pointing the antenna like a water witch around the bedroom in search of his mellifluous murmur in my ear. Tonight a fully developed, sweet-scented girl sat in silence beside me. Praying she would understand the necessity, I switched the car radio on mentally vowing to switch it off the moment I'd learned the game's score.

I don't remember whether the Dodgers won or lost that night. A maddening bunch of bunters and bleeder hitters, they were usually no more successful at reaching base than I. What I do remember is my left ear pressed to the radio, a silvery moon above us, as Vinnie's velvet voice dissolved in static and a pretty girl's face turned as distant as the stars in the prairie sky.

Somehow I eventually managed to find a woman willing to marry me. Two of them, in fact. Though the extent to which my sports obsessions contributed to the failure of my first marriage and continued to color my second was psychic terrain I had never summoned the will to explore prior to this latest return to the little French village in the Dordogne. Like faux pas or incompetence with machinery, it was simply an affliction that seemed to be encoded in the family genes. My youngest brother, who still lived in Nebraska, showed every sign of carrying an even more virulent strain than Doug or I carried. Fortunately he was married to a woman who shared it, which said either that he hit a million-to-one genetic lottery or was far better at touching all the bases than I'd been. Or maybe both. No doubt it helped that he looked like Sting.

And so, Souillac. Sacrificing dinner with Jane and our friends, I'd grabbed the last available chair outside the thronged brasserie on that charged midsummer night seven years earlier, after reluctantly leaving the church an hour before game time. A couple of hundred French fans were already wedged inside the door, fortifying themselves with beer and wine, their chants spilling out onto the sidewalk where I perched giddily. The eyes of all of us were fixed on the single TV above the bar, glowing with images a billion other people were simultaneously viewing around the planet. Soon I too had my game-face on—almost as deeply into it as I'd have been back home with Doug and Scott, watching the Cornhuskers about to get it on with the detested Sooners or Buffs. I wanted France to win not only because they were the underdog, but because I was hooked on their country, and because they'd never won a championship, and maybe most of all because their fans gave off a collective vibe that felt different from any I'd recently experienced back home in the States. More light-hearted, fun-loving, as high-spirited as a World Series or Super Bowl crowd yet seemingly aware that this was, after all, just a game. A big game, yes—without question the biggest in France's national history. Yet still a game for all that, and if they lost, as surely they would, *c'est la vie*. Well into the tense, emotionally draining first half, a pair of young males sitting next to me were far more attentive to their cooing girl friends than they were to the stirring exploits on the field, a phenomenon that back home in Lincoln, on a Saturday afternoon in Memorial Stadium, would have been about as likely as the crowd starting a chant for the A.C.L.U.

When the match ended and France had won, I joined as much as a foreigner can in a nation's elation. Souillac was much too small to reach the blowout heights of Paris or Lyon, but even in its modest environs there was a euphoric, almost childlike, outpouring of joy. Music blared and people danced in the tiny square across from our hotel. Horns honked endlessly. Cars funneling up the narrow street were briefly stopped and rocked by laughing fans, then allowed to creep on as a single blue-capped gendarme watched indulgently, his face spread with a goofy grin. All of it brought back the most thrilling day of my boyhood—grainy black and white images from Brooklyn via the still wondrous magic of television after Johnny Podres shut out the invincible Yankees to give my beloved Bums at last their endlessly delayed World Series crown.

It all seemed a long time ago, even the Souillac of 1998, as I crept down the snow-glazed highway into the little town two days after my experience in Arromanches. But Souillac too at first sight looked much the same as I remembered it. The hotel where we'd stayed the night the French won the Cup was closed for the season, but another one nearby appeared to be open, and the little *boulangeries* and *charcuteries* on the street where the passing cars had been rocked remained open as well. I parked in the square across from the bar where I'd watched the game and walked on to the abbey church, my breath quickening as I approached the tiny leather-covered entrance door, steeling myself for the letdown if it turned out to be locked. When the latch yielded to my hand, I felt a flood of gratitude and walked in.

I stood for a long time in the dim interior, staring at the statue, my reverie broken only by the occasional echo of muted footsteps on the stone floor. An aged priest and a nun were readying the altar for the next service, but I soon forgot them in the rapt absorption the bas-relief inspired. What held me first were the elongated, scissored legs, dramatically crossed in a fluid intersection where motion and stasis flowed together. The muscles of the flank and extended left arm bulged naturalistically beneath the thin cloth that shrouded them. I thought again of an athlete's grace—of Koufax—the arc of his arm across his taut body in classic photos snapped at the moment the ball exploded from his long-fingered hand. I had seen him pitch only once in the flesh, a September night not long after my surfboard fiasco in that Oz-like year I'd lived in southern California. On that occasion too I remembered neither who the Dodgers played nor whether they had won, only that flowing elegance frozen in time, the suppleness of a human body become art.

My gaze drifted lower down the prophet's gown, its folds so delicate the stone was a diaphanous tissue of intricate tracery, then on to the haunting, bearded face mutilated by iconoclasts centuries earlier, their violent erasures paradoxically leaving the vacant eyes even more expressive of a Christ-like compassion and sorrow for a fallen world. Nothing in them was vehement or judgmental, the qualities usually associated with Old Testament prophets, and I felt some of the post-election bitterness I still carried melt away. My church-going days had ended years earlier, but I retained enough residual memory to recognize this was what one was supposed to feel in a place of worship, and my respect for the artist's genius grew even more. I'm not sure how long I stood there in the hypnotic silence, before I suddenly realized I was absolutely alone. The priest and nun had vanished. No one else had entered the sanctuary. Not for the first time in French churches, I felt a shudder course through me at the recognition that, with total impunity, I could have violated one of the world's most exquisite works of art.

It's probably too great a generalizing leap to say that such a moment would never have happened in the United States, where the 9/11 furies had unleashed the full, tragically imperative arsenal of security and surveillance. Or that France had no similar fears, for I knew the previous year's horrific subway bombings in Madrid had sent shock waves throughout the E.U. But I was sure of this—the *feel* of things remained different, the way it had felt not so long ago in America. You sensed it in the smallest French village or the streets of cities as large as Paris. A week earlier I had stood alone and unattended in the *Musée d'Orsay*, gazing at Manet's matchless *Olympia*. On a previous trip it had happened under the famed west portal of Chartres cathedral, which I'd returned to on a midnight run through the city's ancient streets after two hours of insomnia in a wet tent. There too I'd stood alone, mere inches from some of the world's most treasured religious statues, the silence so profound it felt as if I'd been transported to an uninhabited island outside of time. It was that awe I felt again, lingering in the little church in Souillac, gazing on at the Isaiah's ravaged face.

Inevitably, like the tiny farms of Normandy, such experiences would vanish. Many of the changes terrorism had already wrought in my own homeland were surely not far down the road in France. But as I left the abbey—took a last wistful look back down the empty nave at the candlelit altar—I felt only gratitude that this quiet French gift to my spirit had been given once more.

By then it was late afternoon, time to find a place to stay for the night. I walked back down the street past the hotel where my wife and I had stayed on our last visit, confirmed the *"fermeture annuelle"* sign in its window, and walked on to the other I had earlier driven past, a two-story inn marked with a discreet green and yellow hearth I hadn't noticed from the car. The sign was one Jane and I had come to trust, signaling a network of small hotel-restaurants in mostly rural villages throughout the country loosely organized under the rubric *Logis de France*. Each was different, individually owned, the rooms unfailingly clean and moderately priced. And the food—typically a rich variety of regional dishes—rose from the merely succulent to the *ohmigod* divine.

Exhilarated by the discovery, I checked in and returned to the street fixed on the second objective that had drawn me back to Souillac, a goal as quixotic, maybe even lunatic, as the medieval sculpture was sublime. This idea too had taken root seven years earlier, in the town's jubilant celebration of its World Cup victory, years filled with a growing concern over the role sport had come to play in both my native country and my own life. Badly in need of some objective distance, I hoped somehow to find a French sports junkie—a man like myself, if such a person existed—and then take the deepest soundings he would allow me in an attempt to discover how his life compared to mine in the United States.

But where did one begin such an eccentric mission? Asking a hotel owner a few kilometers from Omaha Beach if he knew anyone who'd witnessed the D-Day invasion was one thing, but accosting someone on the street with "*Pardon, monsieur, mais…uh…connaissez-vous quelqu'un qui est un fanatique pour le sport?*" Even my gaucherie threshold didn't stretch that far.

In the end, the problem was solved by another stroke of blind luck. Souillac's appearance had changed very little since my last visit, but fifteen minutes of walking its wintry streets brought me to the edge of town and the sudden, astonishing realization that I was staring at an Irish pub. My reaction was basically what it would have been walking through my nearby village of Hokah, Minnesota, and happening on a *Logis de France*. But there it was, clearly labeled "O'Leary's," with a "*Happy Hour 17-20 heures*" posted above the door. I had never been in an Irish pub in France, but I knew that finding a sports fanatic in one in America was about as difficult as scoring a draught of Guinness. Bounding across the street in gratitude, I turned the heavy iron door handle to walk in.

If the next few seconds turned out to be slightly less humiliating than my barging entry into the Paris restaurant a week earlier, it's only because most people I know would have done the same thing. At four o'clock in the afternoon, you can press any bar door in America and be virtually certain it will yield to your hand. My mistake was momentarily forgetting that this was far from true in France. Knowing the hours when *anything* would be closed or open, in fact, was an enigma of such Byzantine complexity you eventually learned simply not to worry about it—just went with the flow and filled up with gas whenever the gauge dropped low and you saw cars parked by the pumps in a station; bought your croissants when they were available regardless of what past experience suggested about the open hours of *boulangerie*s.

Unfortunately, that cultural memory surfaced only as I reflexively rattled the pub door a few more times. When it suddenly yielded—a split second after I belatedly noticed the small sign indicating that the pub itself, not just its happy hour, opened at five—I cringed with chagrin.

An attractive woman stood staring at me in the doorway, a broom in her braceleted hand. Startled, I mumbled my sheepish litany of "*pardon*"s and "*excusez-moi*"s, which she cut off with an amused smile. Over the next couple of minutes as we stood talking, I learned that she was from Holland, that her name was Monique (courtesy of her Francophile parents), and that she and her Irish husband had opened the pub a couple of years earlier after an aborted attempt to run a nearby campground had failed.

Like nearly all the Dutch I'd ever met, she spoke flawless English, another stroke of good fortune for which I was almost prayerfully grateful. The question I'd spent most of our genial interchange silently working up the nerve to ask her was going to sound weird enough in my native language, God only knew what her reaction would be if I attempted it in French. Apologizing again for intruding on her, I finally risked it. She gazed at me blankly in stupefaction, another faint, incredulous smile eventually creasing her face. It was indeed a "pretty strange" question, she agreed, and I was right—no one had ever asked her anything remotely like it before. Sport was popular in France, but a "sports fanatic"? She knew only one person in Souillac who might fit the description. By chance, he owned a *cave* just up the street from where I stood. Leaning the broom against the wall she stepped abruptly past me, leaving me the one now momentarily taken aback, and led me briskly on a hundred-yard walk to the wine shop's front door. A stocky, athletic-looking Frenchman who appeared to be roughly her age, somewhere in his late thirties, nodded to her as we entered. His name was Jean-Paul, she whispered to me as he turned back to his work.

Two gray-haired and obviously married customers lingered in the comfortable room, deliberating over their choice of table wine, and the Dutchwoman waited with me just inside the doorway as a pair of friendly dogs sniffed at our feet. The wait gave me a chance to ask her a few more questions, and she remained as forthright in her answers as she had been before. She had lived in a number of places around the world, she said—Scotland, New Zealand, several others—and had settled with her husband in Souillac several years earlier. Their French was fluent, but most of their friends, she added a bit ruefully, remained the few other non-natives who lived in the town.

Why was that, I asked.

She looked away for several seconds before answering, following the wine transaction taking place a few feet away.

The French were tight-knit, she eventually answered—very centered on their families. There was a point, despite the town's obvious and genuine graciousness, where it was difficult, maybe impossible, for outsiders to "break through."

I wanted to follow up on this illuminating perspective—which bespoke a genteel clannishness vividly familiar from the prairie villages of my own youth—but the other couple had made their purchase, and after ushering them to the door, the wine merchant stepped nimbly around his dogs to where we stood. It wasn't hard to imagine him on a playing field—I learned later that he'd been a local star at rugby—or to believe Monique's claim as we'd walked over that he was the one "sports nut" she knew. It was less the loose-limbed, slightly pigeon-toed body than a certain gleam in his eyes. They held a little of the ascetic remoteness of the sculpted Isaiah's, something too of what I saw in my own eyes when I looked in a mirror.

The next few seconds swept by quickly—the obligatory cheek kisses as Jean-Paul and Monique greeted each other; her repetition in French of the "pretty strange" question I had asked her; the Frenchman's raised eyebrows, then slow nod and restrained, slightly wary agreement to meet me back in the pub at six. Moments later its owner and I walked back up the street to the door, where I thanked her repeatedly before hurrying back to my hotel room to spend the intervening hour writing out the difficult questions I wanted to ask. I would not normally have done this, having found it more useful in previous interviews to simply let things roll spontaneously, but the wine merchant spoke no English and the thought of troubling Monique any further died in shame the moment it was born.

I took a corner booth in the pub promptly at the appointed time, a pair of happy-hour lagers in front of me. The slope-shouldered Frenchman walked in a short time later, accompanied by two shy young men he introduced as his son Yann and close friend, Romain. Both of them, he said, were skilled soccer players—*futboleurs*—while his own passion had always been rugby. He remained a devoted follower of the national team, he acknowledged briefly, though his own playing career had ended a few years before.

I asked him if he missed it—the playing—and his eyes took on the kind of look any once-decent athlete recognizes forever, whatever his sport or level of skill. My own baseball career had finished with local "town ball" several years after my college playing days were over, my last game ending abruptly when a catcher's errant throw broke my nose on an attempted steal of third base. Tennis and morning runs had partly filled the void, though even in the present, decades later, there were moments when I missed the game acutely. Not even the first breast I ever touched had felt better than a baseball in my hand.

I said nothing of all this to Jean-Paul, no doubt wisely, though the comparison seemed far less vulgar than the opposite—the feel of that rare thing so perfect it sears the heart to its core. In any case, I read enough in those narrowed eyes to know the long runs he said he also took every Monday morning didn't quite give him the *frisson* he'd felt on the rugby pitch. The latter was a sport I knew very little about, beyond a passing awareness that the players referred to themselves as "ruggers," butted heads in a mad melee called a "scrum," and that a few days earlier the French national team had eked out an apparently dramatic tournament game with its major rival England by a score of nineteen to seventeen. I'd chanced on the last fact in the *International Herald-Tribune*, and hoping it might break down his reserve a bit, I laid my written list of questions momentarily aside. Mentioning the French victory, I asked what it, and the game in general, meant to him; how his wife felt about his involvement; and above all, though I knew this might be difficult to answer, what it was specifically when he played or watched a sport that he loved the most.

The Frenchman's guarded expression softened noticeably. *Bien sûr*, he said, *le sport* had a large place in his life—he'd played it since he was a small boy and still watched many rugby and *futbol* matches; *non*, his wife had no problem at all with the time and energy he devoted to it; *oui*, my last question was indeed *difficile*, but if he had to name only one or two things, what he enjoyed most in any sport played uncommonly well were the quick intelligence and remarkable skill of the players. And finally, a mischievous grin flashing briefly on his lean face as he stared at me across the table, the French team had beaten England *eighteen* to seventeen.

All in all, I thought, not much different from what I'd have expected from a passionate Husker or Vikings fan back in my own country, with a single, striking exception. (I didn't express my private doubts, bred of painful personal experience, about his wife's unquestioning support of his obsessions. If true, I attributed it to the different universe that was French television: when I told him I sometimes watched three successive football games on Sundays—close to ten consecutive hours as a couch potato—his eyes widened in disbelief. Such a thing was impossible in France, he said.)

The exception was the answer he'd given when I asked what it was about sport that engaged him most. The qualities he cited—the quick thinking and uncommon prowess of the athletes—ranked highest for me as well, but felt increasingly out of synch with the brute strength and "in your face" physical violence that so often juiced American stadiums to their most primal roars. Too often to count in recent years, I'd heard the breathtaking athleticism of a Pete Sampras or the deft footwork of international soccer icons dismissed as "boring"; seen the brains-over-brawn style of unselfish teams like the San Antonio Spurs draw TV ratings markedly lower than those garnered by teams more inclined to basketbrawls; and marveled at the swelling fan base in dirt-filled arenas where monster vehicles slammed the earth and each other with ear-shattering force. The sense of loss, from old world to new, was profound. Unsure how to do it, I wanted to probe the Frenchman's thoughts on the change.

Less than a month before I left on the trip, my home-state Vikings had lost a hard-fought playoff game to the Eagles in Philadelphia, where supporters of the Minnesota team had reportedly been spit on, physically threatened, and showered with beer. Sitting in that French bar, remembering the light-hearted outpouring of joy I'd witnessed after the World Cup victory, I felt my stomach tighten at the inevitable comparisons. The wine merchant obviously wasn't attuned to sport in my country, though he knew who had won the Super Bowl and seemed familiar with the basics of American football. I described to him the crowd behavior in Philadelphia and a few equally notorious recent examples of U.S. sports mania, from hockey bloodlettings to angry parents verbally and even physically assaulting coaches and umpires over their kids' games. Did such things ever happen in France, I asked. No, he shook his head, never—then reconsidered when his son spoke up for the first time, sitting quietly but attentively at his side. Yes, the wine merchant backtracked slightly, something like that might happen in one instance—when Paris played Marseilles in *futbol*—but only then, and always outside the stadium. During the game the two teams' fans sat in separate sections, and he'd never heard of such behavior anywhere else in France.

Yann's brief input was the first indication I had that he spoke English.

Noticing my look of gratitude, Jean-Paul smiled and abruptly turned toward a row of people perched on stools at the bar. "*Alex*," he called. A young woman, her intelligent eyes and thick dark hair accented by a stylish plum-colored scarf, hopped down and walked over to where we sat. He introduced her as Alexandra, Yann's girlfriend. She was eighteen, and had spent her childhood in Manchester, England. For the kinds of additional questions I hoped to raise, having someone fluent in both languages at the table was a potential godsend, and I asked her to join us. Standing, Jean-Paul cleared his place for her, adding with a cryptic smile that he hadn't finished his work back at the *cave* and had to leave. Seconds later, thanking me for the beer, he shook my hand firmly and walked out the door.

The abrupt departure briefly threw me, though nothing he'd said or done during our short conversation had suggested the Frenchman's stated reason wasn't genuine—that he'd grown bored, or perhaps uncomfortable with the questions he might have sensed I was about to ask. But there was no way to know for sure. I knew only that our parting felt congenial, and that the three students who remained in the booth appeared willing to continue the conversation—seemed eager in fact to sustain it. Unsure now myself where we were headed, I discarded the suddenly useless list of written questions and decided to press on.

I returned at once to the subject I had raised just before the vintner's departure, charged with uneasy significance in either language—*violence*. The accents and pronunciations were different but the word was the same. The three teen-agers glanced at each other and nodded. It was dishearteningly clear that my fixation on the topic didn't surprise them. I was an American. The 60's-era axiom that flashed inevitably through my own brain they would almost certainly not have recognized, though the truth behind it was transparent on their faces: *violence was as American as apple pie.*

It was the young woman who responded first.

"When you think of the United States," she said in English, "you think of everything big...and of violence. We feel it's very...I don't know...very strange."

I told her that though I'd lived in America all my life our numb tolerance of it felt more and more strange to me too, the more time I spent in European societies. My own state of Minnesota had recently passed a law allowing people to carry concealed weapons, I added. It wasn't uncommon to see signs posted in stores and public buildings banning entry with a handgun, much as the slanted red diagonal over a cigarette banned smoking in the corner of the bar where we sat. The look that spread across her face was one of stunned disbelief.

I had come to France in part to hear what its people thought of my country, but the students' ensuing silence said more than words could. While I wasn't surprised they were shocked, the depth of aversion in their faces rattled me. Glancing down at the useless notes, I moved on. What were their general impressions of the United States, I asked. "It's a country with a very powerful economy," Alex was again the one who responded, Romain nodding vigorously in agreement. *Mondovino* still fresh in my memory, I asked them if they saw the U.S. as a threat to their own country's economic future—to small businesses like the wine *cave* owned by Yann's dad. "Everything follows America," Alex answered. French businesses were no different. The corporate power of the United States was intimidating, even a little frightening. More and more the big *supermarchés* were popular. A large *Leclerc* store had recently been built on the edge of Souillac. "A lot of little companies are fading away," she said.

It was exactly what Pierre Affre had told me in Paris, and the confirmation was depressing enough I changed the subject once more. Since the straightforward young woman had spent her early childhood in England, I asked for her impressions of the French town that had been her home ever since. "It feels like you're living fifty years ago," she responded immediately, the words echoing my own feelings so closely they were startling from the lips of one so young. "Sometimes it's too slow," she added, "but you get used to it."

Neither she nor her boyfriend expressed any desire to escape to a city, the feeling so common among small-town youth in the United States, though Romain said he would like to visit America sometime because he preferred larger places. "And when you think of America, that's what you think of—the cities," Alex interjected, volunteering a translation of his next sentence for me. Her economics teacher had told them the educational opportunities in the U.S. were greater than in their own country, she added, especially if you wanted to do research, as she did. "I might go there just for that reason," she said. "It's hard for anybody to advance in France, it's so laid back." Her words recalled for me a quote I'd recently read from Nicolas Sarkozy, the conservative French interior minister who would soon become the nation's next President. "The dream of French families is that their children go to American universities," he'd told an audience in New York City. It was, at that moment in the little Souillac pub, a much needed reminder of those brighter things about my country that had helped earn its reputation as a beacon to the world.

Glancing at the bar, I phrased the next question as delicately as I could, uncertain whether to raise it at all. Taking care not to compromise my source, I said I'd recently been told that outsiders found it difficult to penetrate the close-knit fabric of French village life, even when they'd lived in the country for some time. The young woman born in England looked briefly surprised, then shook her head dismissively. "I think it's mainly in things like sports," she laughed. Pressing her gently, I asked if there were ways the observation fit other areas as well. No, she shook her head again, her brow furrowing. Souillac was definitely tight-knit—she repeated her earlier comment about feeling like you'd been dropped back into the past—but it was a life that appealed to her personally. "In France you live by solidarity," she finished with a flourish. "Whereas in England, and especially America, I think you work for yourself."

She was eighteen, had never been to the United States, and the generalization had the glib conviction only the young or the terminally Manichaean give voice to. Yet it reinforced enough of my own empirical impressions I decided to risk the last question I'd written in the hotel room—had put at the end of the list for fear it might permanently chill the atmosphere if I raised it before.

"You know I'm from the U.S.," I said, pausing to look across the table into each of their faces, "but I'd like you to answer this next question as honestly as you can." I paused again and waited for a reaction, the words hanging in the air, hoping that same impulsive adolescent frankness might divulge feelings that had been suppressed in my earlier conversations with people older and more circumspect. When all three eventually nodded, glancing at each other uncertainly, I went on.

"What do you think of Americans," I said—"the American *people*, not the country itself?"

Predictably, the self-assured Alex responded first, rendered a verdict that was just as predictable. "I think Americans are artificial," she said, glancing again at her boyfriend, whose guarded, luminous eyes remained fixed on mine. From the beginning, he had been the quietest of the three, a remarkably good-looking, dark-haired youth whose polite reserve was as compelling as it was a mirror of his father's. I was particularly interested in his impressions, for the few words he'd voiced in the hour I'd sat across from him had all seemed thoughtful and mature. Finally he spoke. "I think Americans are vulgar," he said softly, his eyes holding on mine.

However predictable this might have been too, a judgment I'd encountered so often in Henry James and countless continental writers it had come to have the musty feel of cliché, the indictment still saddened me, beyond whatever personal edge it may have held. The word he'd chosen was another of thousands common to both cultures—the French from was *vulgaire*—and my mind flashed over its shifting range of meanings: *common, lewd and indecent, coarse*. The only thing clear in the next slow, painful seconds was that the two other students agreed with him. I asked if they felt the same about people from North America in general—about Canadians, for example—and they all said no.

Then Alex went further. She had seen *Fahrenheit 9/11*, she said, and knew several other people in Souillac who had also seen it. The movie was quite widely known in France. A few of the scenes seemed a bit exaggerated, she added, but most of it only confirmed what people already suspected about the United States. I asked what impression she had of the President who had just been elected to a second term. "It's like he came out of another film—*Independence Day*"—she answered. "It's hard to take him seriously...but you have to. We all do."

The table again fell silent, before the young woman once more expressed her dismay at the pervasive violence in my country, adding that she was particularly upset by "the death sentence"—her term for capital punishment. France was different, she said. "You're not really scared here." The words hung like a knife in the air as the four of us sat staring at each other, the click of pool balls echoing from the next room. There was nothing more I could think of to ask them, or at least nothing more that in those longer moments of awkward silence I felt inclined to. Rising, I thanked them for both their patience with me and their admirable candor, and walked back to the hotel.

But my thoughts remained back in the pub, on the oppressive fact that three French teenagers seemed saner and more knowledgeable about the things that counted than my own President and the arrogant zealots who had brought my country to such an isolated place in the world. I hadn't told Alex that during his term as governor of Texas, Mr. Bush had presided over 152 executions, more than any other executive in America's recent history, or that his legal counsel at the time, now the nation's chief law enforcer as Attorney General, had said the nature of the "war on terror" had rendered "obsolete" the Geneva conventions, which he called "quaint."

My mood had turned as dark as the winter sky. Walking on, I thought again of Twain—of the yawning gulf between his boyhood love of a land so brilliantly captured in Huck's eloquent dawn-songs on the river and his revulsion at the barbarism, greed, and demagoguery of "sivilization." Thought of his own rage at the country's imperialistic forays into weaker nations and its remarkable capacity for self-deceit. I remembered the stricken look on Alex's face when I'd mentioned the laws permitting concealed weapons, Jean-Paul's only slightly less disbelieving reaction when I told him of sometimes spending an entire Sunday afternoon and evening staring at football games on TV. None of it was flattering, to my country or to myself. I regretted the fact I'd said nothing in praise of my still beloved homeland's virtues, the deeply embedded qualities I knew lived on in its people, ripe for leaders with more soul and clearer sight.

I ate alone that night in the *Logis*, the *confit de canard* and fifteen-euro *menu* as good as I'd hoped, then returned to my room and drifted into a broken sleep charged with the day's events. Something was missing, remained a disconnect between the pair of things that had drawn me back to Souillac—some linkage long felt but still subconscious that had fused a boyhood baseball hero with a medieval statue and flowed so deeply through my native culture it had surfaced in an obsessive love of sports. I felt I had glimpsed it in the wine merchant as well, and in his son. Felt it flash briefly in the father's eyes when he mentioned the boy's prowess as a *futboleur*. It was the look of my own father, and my grandfather too, watching me play.

I was no great shakes as a baseball player, in the wry prairie vernacular of that distant era, but in the close to thirty years I'd followed my bliss on scruffy, sun-baked diamonds neither of them had missed more than a handful of my games. The image of my grandfather's hunched frame leaning forward in the bleachers rose with vivid clarity in my memory, his jaw clenching a cigar stub and his eyes burning beneath a grease-stained seed cap, the depth of his emotional investment in my play nearly as palpable as the dirt under my spikes. My games meant everything to him, or seemed to—meant so much I often played tight and felt pressured despite the fact an occasional "Attaboy!" or "*Pull* the ball!" were the only voiced utterances that escaped his grizzled throat.

Years later, after his death, my aunt told me what it had been like to live in the Dust Bowl during the Depression. Barely into her teens then, his daughter described as if it were yesterday the inch of grit that covered everything in the house after the wind-driven black clouds had swept over them across the prairie; the ache of sweeping up for hours, then scrambling again to close the windows in the scorching heat as yet another dark mass loomed in the southern sky. She told of my father putting cardboard in his shoes to cover the holes in the soles; of once peeking at the family account book and discovering the month's allotment for groceries was eight dollars; of cutting so close to the bone they'd made their own soda crackers, sewed her skirts out of old handkerchiefs, taken bushels of wheat several miles to a makeshift mill for the flour that would reduce the cost of their bread. My grandmother had done the weekly laundry in front of the house using tubs and a scrubboard, my aunt told me, boiling the water on the kitchen stove and carrying it down the stoop in smaller buckets. My father had walked five miles to a hayfield and back for the single dollar he earned working a twelve-hour day for another farmer. When her own shoes wore through she'd had to wear a discarded pair of her mother's, their heels sawed off in the vain hope of making them less an object of adolescent ridicule. Walking the two miles to and from the school pulling a wagon in the winter, she had delivered milk from their three cows to Clarks townspeople, picking up the empty bottles on her return home that night.

Neither my grandfather nor my dad had ever mentioned any of it to me. Or rather, they had touched only on the lighter side that she also described, her voice swelling still with the remembered joy of it—eating corn on the cob and fresh garden tomatoes every summer weekday; the grateful delight they took in a fried chicken dinner on Sunday; half-mile hikes down to the Platte in the evenings to duck beneath the shallow water and cool off. But on that restless night in Souillac, groping for the link I had missed, I felt the full reach of my aunt's description in a way I never had before—felt it all flow together—the quiet austerity of a Romanesque sculpture, men whose emotions lay buried so deep only sports could channel them to the surface, and a peerless athlete whose economy of motion and tightly guarded privacy had made him unique in twentieth-century sport.

Even as a young man, I recognized how odd it was that Sandy Koufax had become my hero. A Jew from Brooklyn, he inhabited a sphere of American experience as distant from my own as it was possible to get. But not until that night in the French hotel did I grasp the reasons for his lifelong hold on me, beyond his amazing feats for the team I'd worshipped as a boy. A degenerative, arthritic elbow had ended his career in its prime. With the help of cortisone shots his last few seasons, he'd pitched through pain so intense his arm had to be sheathed in ice for an hour after each game to numb it, yet posted one of the most glittering records his final five years in the history of the Major Leagues. Through it all he maintained the same quiet dignity and sense of perspective that had once led him to sacrifice a scheduled World Series opening start because it fell on the sacred Jewish holy day Yom Kippur. And in the decade following his sadly abrupt retirement in the mid-60's, already an age when even the iconic Joe DiMaggio could succumb to the siren song of easy pitchman's money from Mr. Coffee and corporate banks, the Dodger lefthander had simply vanished from the American landscape, passing up millions for a life of such quiet seclusion he lived for a time on a remote New England farm.

I felt it all that night—the remarkable power, and the mystery, of suppressed emotion. To the day of their deaths, I never heard my grandfather swear, or saw my father cry, or heard either of them express the kinds of feelings those countless baseball and football games had channeled. Whatever their private rages, disappointments, and sorrows, sports alone had made them acceptable to public view. The loudest sounds I ever heard escape my father's throat came from his end zone seat in Memorial Stadium during tense games when the Huskers were losing; the single unbridled cry of exultation I remember my grandfather voicing was a celebration of the team's dramatic defeat of Oklahoma in the fabled "Game of the Century" in 1971.

Psychologists would no doubt call such emotional reticence unhealthy, not least to the women and children constrained to live daily in its wake. As their son and grandson, I knew I would go to my own grave unaware how either of those two most formative men in my life felt about death, or sex, or the possible non-existence of God. Somewhere near the root of that hard prairie legacy surely lay at least part of the answer to "What's the matter with Kansas?"—the paradoxical fact that the Plains remained a Republican stronghold even as the party's plutocratic, elitist leadership dealt blow after fatal blow to the small farms and villages at the region's cultural heart. Gritty self-denial—that same fierce, tight-lipped independence that had served it so well through years of drought and Depression—had too often become a knee-jerk scorn for a democratic inclusiveness that would benefit all but the greediest, had warped the once-shrewd distrust of con men and glib snake-oil salesmen into a reflexive blindness to the shameless demagoguery of the far right.

But it was not those darker things that stuck as I lay in the darkness of the French hotel room. It was a medieval statue, and the sport I loved best, and the still not quite fully plumbed connection between them. "I'm always saying something that's just the edge of something more," the most commonly misread poet in my literary experience had once asserted. It seemed as good a definition of poetry, maybe of what we call art, as any, especially those works that most stirred the soul. Five years earlier, at a writer's conference in New England, I'd left my dormitory room at dawn every morning to run two miles through the woods to the isolated cabin of the deceased old laureate whose thorny, deceptively melodic lyrics could chafe your consciousness for days after you'd read them. As could the frost heave of remarks like the one cited above, or his cracker-barrel observation "I never feel more at home in America than at a ball game."

I drove out of Souillac at dawn the next morning, slowing to take a last look at the twelfth-century church. Early in our interview, in the free-wheeling set of questions when his eyes had gleamed the brightest, I had asked Jean-Paul what the statue of Isaiah meant to him. He stared at me penetratingly for several seconds, his face a mask, the air filling with the awkward fact that he had never seen it. Or possibly that he had, but simply hadn't noticed the sculpture was there. The region had a long and turbulent history of anti-clericalism, the iconoclastic scars still etched violently on the prophet's sad visage, and I didn't push the question further. It was "just for tourists," he finally answered, the two young men beside him nodding in agreement. None of them appeared aware that nearly a millennium earlier an anonymous genius had created a work of such haunting grace and beauty it could still draw mesmerized pilgrims from hundreds of kilometers distant to stand reverently at its foot. The church was less than four hundred yards from the pub where we'd sat talking, three generations of sport-loving males on separate stages of life's swift journey. At that moment I felt very close to them, and very far away.

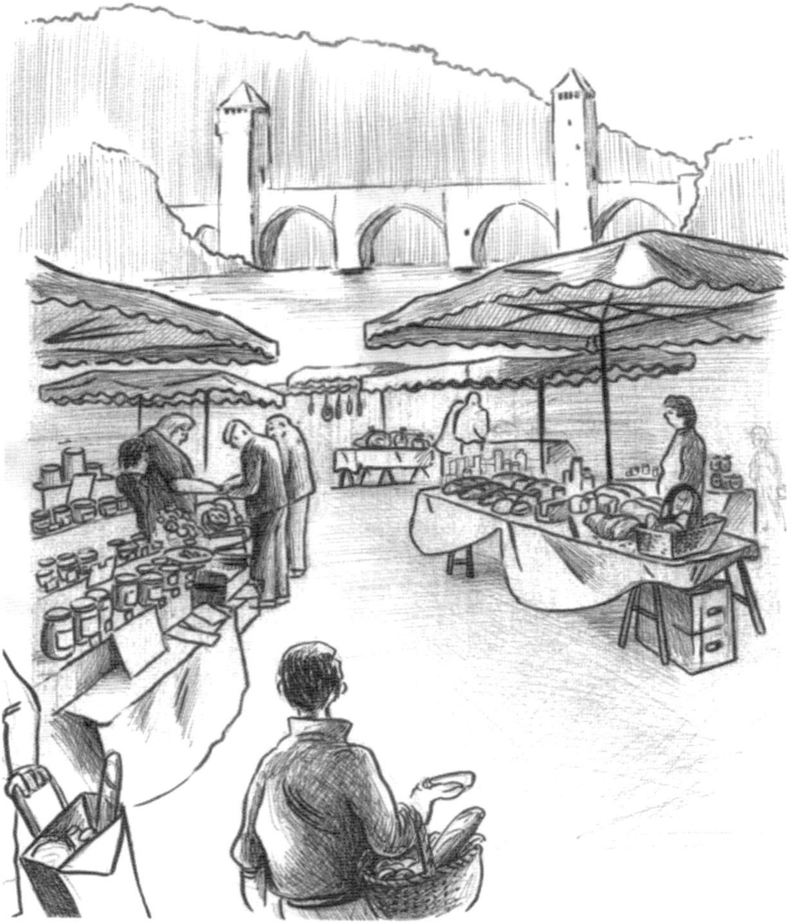

Chapter 5
Bridges

Narrow medieval streets. White limestone cliffs and jet-dark wine from some of the country's most picturesque villages. The ancient Pont Valentré, a fortified stone span arching over the River Lot since the fourteenth century, built to repel the English during the Hundred Years War. There were a lot of things pulling me back to the walled town of Cahors, on the southern edge of the Dordogne. One of them was urgent enough it roused me out of my Souillac hotel bed before dawn.

French food markets had captivated me from the moment I first strolled through one, and Cahors had the most seductive I'd ever seen. I didn't know if it too dated back to the Middle Ages, like so much else I found beguiling about the town—only that it had long been a fixed presence every Saturday morning in the stone square below the cathedral where Jane and I had chanced on it seven years before. The memory, a ravishing of all five senses, had fueled my early morning Souillac departure. Cahors was almost a hundred kilometers distant, and a winter storm blanketing the northern half of the country had already turned the sky an ominous gray as I drove uneasily on.

When the road curved sharply down into the river valley and the red tile roofs of the town finally emerged through the spitting snow, my grip relaxed a bit on the steering wheel. The only question now was whether an outdoor market would be held in such weather. Trusting its long history, I drove on toward the *centre ville*, warmed by its dour charm. Virtually everything about the place felt old—the squat, earth-colored buildings, cramped warren of winding streets, and the dark, born-of-the-soil faces of the people. When I passed a shawled woman carrying an empty wicker basket and walking briskly in the direction of the cathedral, I knew the market was on despite the snow.

Squeezing into a just-vacated space among the rows of other vehicles wedged along the river, I walked the quarter-mile back to the bustling square and fell at once under its spell, the ageless mystique of the *terroir*—that elastic, untranslatable term the French use for everything I saw in front of me. Settling reflexively into my market rhythm, I drifted from stall to canopied stall as perhaps only the unhurried traveler with no objective but total immersion in the experience can. The assault on the senses was as irresistible as I remembered. Though the trunk of my tiny car was already stuffed close to capacity with luggage, I couldn't pass the rich pâtes and multi-colored cheeses, the farm-made *saucissons* and gleaming jars of honey—row after fragrant row of heaped nuts and patisserie tartes and fresh-baked *baguettes* stacked neatly beside *boules* and *ficelles* and the still bewitching, jet-black local wine. The veil of falling snow over the wet brick square brushed it all with the gauzy feel of an Impressionist painting, casting a soft glaze over the market's blue and yellow canopies, its sheltered roses and marigolds in full bloom.

"*Produits du terroir.*" You saw the signs everywhere, driving the byways of rural France, and increasingly in the *supermarchés* of its towns and cities. Five minutes in that Cahors market would have removed the bewilderment, and possibly much of the anger, felt in America and other nations over the country's fierce, self-protective stance on tariffs and farm subsidies. They had made France the latest *bête noire* of international trade negotiations—reached a level of intransigence that would soon influence the nation's stubborn rejection of the proposed E.U. Constitution. But if you talked to the French themselves, the resistance was far less about trade issues than a deep-seated concern over a threatened way of life.

Even in the chill of winter, the Cahors market made it hard to be critical of the French view. I hadn't lived through the grim Depression years my aunt had so vividly described to me, when the family's precarious economic survival hung on the meager crops they raised and the produce from their large garden, but the latter had been a fixed presence through every summer of my childhood, though with none of the nostalgic pull it held now. Back then, our garden meant only that my back hurt and blisters creased my hands after two hours of weeding rows of stringbeans and potatoes. Garter snakes slithered through the asparagus. Mosquitoes harried my face and arms whenever I was sent out to the shaded strawberry patch behind the garage. Only later did I come to appreciate what my aunt's memory had also tangibly evoked—how great all that home-grown food had tasted compared to the generic, industrially grown produce found in most of today's supermarkets. It wasn't the Depression, but I too had eaten fresh-plucked corn on the cob and juicy tomatoes at virtually every evening meal from mid-July through early September. An old couple who lived next door, the Imhoffs, kept a single cow in their small barn and carried its milk into their screen porch, where they ran it through a gleaming metal separator. It was never a chore to leave that bug-infested strawberry patch to watch them finish and hand the aproned Mrs. Imhoff the fifty-cent piece my mother had given me for a pint of fresh cream.

The Cahors market flung me happily back to that remote time, its brusque but cheerful vendors the swarthy farmers and regional artisans who had raised or baked or gathered the sprawling palette that contrasted so sharply with the "tasteless, colorless sameness" of the American traveler's typical fare, now considerably more tasteless than that Steinbeck had described. Gradually the mesh bag I'd brought swelled to overflowing. Still I ambled on, following my nose to a secluded little stall where a shrimp-and-chorizo laced, yard-wide pan of paella bubbled and steamed. The carry-away containers came in three sizes. Barely suppressing a gluttonous urge for the largest, I pointed to the middle one and stood spellbound watching the gypsy-featured vendor heap it high with the savory contents, then fled the market before my crumbling defenses yielded to anything more.

All of it reminded me again why I had fallen in love with provincial France, continued to be so taken by it, and I drove only a few kilometers down the narrow winding road beyond the town's ancient walls before pulling over to park along the riverbank once more. It too felt hauntingly familiar, drawing me even further back in time. Among my earliest childhood memories was the hypnotic purl of rivers—of gazing out at the interlace of sand and silvery currents from the bridge across the Platte in my home village, at the quiet flow of the Republican past our willow-woven duck blind in the fall.

Spreading a towel over my lap, I slowly ate the paella, gazing out at the slate-colored water and the pale cliffs rising dramatically above. Just downstream, the fortified Pont Valentré remained where it had been built in the Middle Ages. A few miles up the road in the opposite direction lay the prehistoric cave paintings at Pêche-Merle. The car's solitude deepened the revery that had settled on me like the snow, which continued to fall. When Jane and I had toured the cave where the paintings had been found, we'd stood transfixed over the footprint of a Cro-Magnon, its outline so distinct in the calcified mud it might have been made five minutes before.

Mesmerized by the river's flow, I ate another slow mouthful of the paella and thought of other bridges, across generations and cultures and glinting stretches of water I would never see. And of those that I would. One of them was barely twenty miles distant, spanned by the narrowest bridge I had ever driven across, and finishing the last satisfying bites of the food, I drove on.

Bouzies. The village's name remained as intoxicating as the little vineyards one passed on the scenic route toward it, driving or biking the region's strikingly diverse terrain. A riverside *Logis* lay tucked at its edge, at the base of a snaking road that wound five kilometers up the cliffs to an even more euphonious village, *St. Cirq-Lapopie.* You reached both sites over the wee little bridge so narrow you had to turn the car off the highway at close to a right angle to cross it. In the summer, when the region bustled with tourists, strings of vehicles sometimes stacked up at both ends of its single lane waiting their turn.

The memory briefly made me glad it was February, a gratitude that swelled again when I reached Bouzies a half-hour later and found an almost ghostlike absence of activity, the unchanged little *pont* now even more a picture postcard through the falling snow.

But as I'd feared, the *Logis* where we'd stayed on the opposite bank of the river was closed. Nothing that moved, human or otherwise, was visible in the village. I knew there was even less chance of finding a hotel open in St. Cirq, but I threaded the car across the tiny bridge and drove on up the winding road to the clifftop site anyway, still more than glad to sacrifice the summer throngs for an environment so pristine. The great Wisconsin naturalist Aldo Leopold had called it "contrast value"—the heightened intensity that comes through the kinship of opposites—the fact that pleasure, to cite the most obvious example, is knowable only if one is familiar with pain. Rarely had the term's elemental wisdom registered the way it did during the next half-hour, as I trudged the lovely little village's empty streets through a two-inch slush that left my feet soaked and half-frozen, the price I willingly paid for a last-minute decision before the trip to save luggage space by leaving my snow boots behind.

A more dramatic trade-off in the wintry weather was an isolated, panoramic view of the distant river, not a souvenir stand or postcard carousel anywhere in sight. I'd walked nearly the full length of the village, in fact, before finally encountering another human, an old man who stood peering out from the front step of his stone house like a groundhog checking the conditions before settling back into his burrow for two or three more weeks of snug rest. Sloshing to a stop, I hailed him and asked if he knew of anyplace I could find a room. No, he slowly shook his head, pondering. There were only two *auberges* in St. Cirq, he said, and both were closed for the season. He knew of nothing open anywhere near.

Contrast value, I repeated to myself, slogging back to my car. The view remained stunning, and I drove only a few hundred more feet down the empty road out of the village before pulling off at the first overlook I reached. The snow had gradually ceased, and a veil of steam now shrouded the river hundreds of yards below me, the limestone cliffs etched an ethereal white under the slate-gray sky. Because I'd risen so early to reach the Cahors market, I'd missed the morning run I usually took to get the body's juices flowing, and as I lingered there, rapt at the valley's beauty, I made another snap decision and retrieved my exercise gear from the trunk. It was five winding kilometers to Bouzies, every step of it downhill, a rare opportunity. The walk back up would be more arduous, but no less picturesque and almost certainly free of all but an occasional passing vehicle. Stripping off my wet clothes in *au naturel* solitude,

I set off. When I got back to the car an hour and a half later, I had still seen no one but the old man at his door.

I stayed that night in a *Logis* halfway between the Pêche-Merle caves and Cahors, on the shores of a gin-clear trout stream whose icy waters flowed just below my room's snow-blanketed balcony. It was another picture-postcard location, and held the promise of a further enticement I'd chanced on earlier in the afternoon. A few kilometers back up the highway, passing through a hamlet of fewer than five hundred residents, I'd glimpsed a small banner draped over the road that appeared to read "*St. Géry. Marché, dimanche.*"

The next morning, sipping coffee in the streamside dining room, I asked the owner about it. Could such a tiny village really have a Sunday morning market, and in the middle of the winter? She was as skeptical as I was. She had never heard of a *marché* in St. Géry, she said, at any time of year. Nonetheless, after seriously pondering the tempting chance to fish the fetching stream with my still unused portable fly-rod before thoughts of its sub-freezing temperatures brought me to my senses, I drove back to the village on the off-chance the banner had said what I thought it did. And the market was in fact there, though compared to the one I'd reveled in twenty-four hours earlier, it was what my dwarfish Peugeot was to a Rolls-Royce.

Still, it was a *marché*, and I was immediately delighted by it—eight or ten canvas-covered stalls displaying fruits and vegetables and several more of the region's singular wines. A handful of vendors stood bundled under the awnings. Barely that many more customers shuffled past them in heavy coats, shopping baskets in hand.

Though outdoor markets had largely vanished in rural America even by the time of my childhood, something in the people's faces felt instantly, unmistakably familiar. The pair of prairie villages I'd grown up in were as tiny as this one, and these were clearly farmers—local townspeople and village merchants—people whose livings were made from the soil or from those who worked it with their calloused hands. Every Saturday through the 1950's, summer or winter, the stores of Silver Creek had stayed open until close to midnight for just such a communal mix of shopping and the week's gossip. At sundown during the summer months, the kids and a few adults drifted on to the town park for ten-cent popcorn and the merchant-sponsored "free show"—usually The Three Stooges followed by a shoot-'em-up western beamed from a rickety projection booth onto a sheet of white canvas lashed to a wooden frame. Except for their winter clothes, the people I passed in that little French market would not have looked out of place in a photograph of the scene, fifty years before.

Moving down the row of stalls, I soon arrived at the end, where a few bottles of wine stood untended on a foldout table. The unoccupied space wasn't surprising. So few people were out in the frigid weather several of the vendors had deserted their stations, stood talking impassively in a patch of pallid sunlight by the street. I was about to return to my car when a woman in the next booth called out to the unaware vintner, and he trudged dutifully back to his stand. I soon learned that his name was Michel Dols. His wife, who joined us a few seconds later and spoke some halting English, was named France. Their sixty hectares of land—about 150 acres—lay a few kilometers to the east, not far from Bouzies, they told me amiably. In addition to the vines, they raised a little corn and wheat, the husband said, but most of their income came from the vineyard and a vine nursery whose plants they sold to other *vignobles* nearby.

It probably goes without saying, though I'd love to be corrected, that there are few if any vineyards in the middle of Nebraska. Yet everything about the couple held me back in time, as if I'd returned to the life I'd known as a child on the American plains. Both sets of my grandparents had been farmers, and among my favorite childhood memories were summer days spent playing in the vacant haymows of their dilapidated old barns, or rummaging dustily through lye-scented washhouses and slatted chicken coops. I told the Dols only that I'd grown up and still lived in farm country in the middle of America, and that I'd be delighted to buy a bottle of their wine.

Michel, a stocky man in late middle age with a florid face set off by his bulky, hooded coat and gray stocking cap, nodded and reached back into their small panel truck for a glass. He poured a sample of the vintage on the table and I found it terrific for the price, a mere four euros a bottle—a rich and earthy *rouge* with enough tannin my thoughts flashed immediately back to *Mondovino*, the threat posed by the milder, micro-oxygenated corporate varietals being pushed so aggressively around the globe.

I asked them if they'd seen the film. No, they shook their heads, but they knew about it. Their son Vincent, in fact, a young oenologue who had studied for eight months in the Napa Valley, had once briefly apprenticed under Michel Rolland, the chauffeur-driven Bordeaux wine buyer and corporate agent for the expanding Mondavi and Rothschild empires. It was his condescending view of peasants as hicks that had grated on me throughout the film. The coincidence was startling enough I risked a further question of the Dols, hoping it wouldn't strike them as an invasion of privacy. What did your son think of Monsieur Rolland, I asked blandly, trying not to convey the scathing perspective on his work I'd taken from the film and the article on it in the *Times*. The two glanced at each other, and the Frenchman gave that wry, what-can-you-say shrug a traveler in the country soon comes to recognize as an inimitable Gallic signature. It's all a matter of taste, he said in French, nodding at the row of bottles on his table. Tastes change. What can one do?

They were clearly too discreet to say more, but one thing became disturbingly apparent as I continued to chat with them. The French wine industry was in crisis—"*en crise,*" as the vintner put it softly. There were many reasons, his wife added in broken English—the changing international tastes, a depressed economy, the recent vigorous campaign to lower public alcohol consumption because the government thought "too much people drinking too much over the roads."

Once again, the Gallic shrug, the "*c'est comme ça.*"

I knew almost nothing about vineyards, the private lives of the people who owned them, but far too much about the hardships faced by small farmers of any age or place. For nearly two decades, from the time I began as a sixteen-year-old trainee under my father until I finally quit the seasonal job the year I was granted tenure at the university where I taught, I had spent much of every summer working as an insurance adjuster of crops damaged by hail. The income paid most of my way through college and graduate school, and the chance to work out in the open air, at least when I first began in the late 1950's, made the repetitive and sometimes awkward nature of the work easier to bear. What became harder to deal with, as the years passed, was the rapid growth of the high-intensity farming my friend Ed had described when I'd called him after his heart attack. Both the typical farm acreages and the machinery got exponentially bigger and more expensive, the corn rows narrower and more heavily laced with potent chemicals, and the small landholders, with whom I'd worked almost exclusively at the beginning, more and more scarce and beaten down. I'd quit the work primarily because my career as a college teacher no longer afforded sufficient time to perform my academic duties well if I continued adjusting, but the breaking point had come one scorching July afternoon when I staggered out of a corn field, watery-eyed and wheezing, from the wind-drifted pesticide a crop duster had dropped on the field across the road.

The memory flitted bat-like across my mind as I continued to converse with the French couple, though this too I didn't mention to them. Yes, the vintner said, a farm meant "*beaucoup de travail*," and the future could never be certain. It was like "*la bourse*," his wife added stoically—the stock market. When we sell the wine, we buy more plants for the nursery. One never knows from one month to the next.

But you're making a decent living at it? I said hopefully. "*Vous gagnez la vie?*" Again the Gallic shrug. They made almost nothing off the wheat and corn, Michel said, and only a modest income off their wine. It was the vine nursery that had turned out best for them, and they hoped it would continue to produce, despite *la crise*.

Though no other customers had approached in the ten minutes or more we'd stood talking, I'd clearly taken far more of their time than the purchase of a single bottle of wine justified. The next question would be my last.

How long have you owned your land? I said.

Michel flashed a pleased smile and pointed to the neatly printed card he'd handed me with the bottle. The first sentence read "*Depuis 130 ans, le domaine Dols cultive la vigne.*" A hundred and thirty years. But that was only the vineyard, France added. The name "Dols" went back hundreds of years earlier—"it means 'from the

Lot country' in the old language," she said proudly—and Michel's family had lived on the same piece of land for too many of those centuries to count. I said nothing in response, merely nodded in quiet appreciation, my mind filled with the silent hope that their son and his descendants might somehow sustain the tradition for hundreds more.

Finally I turned to leave, thanking both of them earnestly, but the vintner raised a calloused palm and murmured a *"moment."* Reaching back again into the little truck, he lifted a bottle of white wine out of a wooden crate and handed it to me. *"Un cadeau,"* he said, a warm smile creasing his round face once more.

Moved by their kindness, I mumbled several additional *"merci beaucoup"*s for the spontaneous gift, then a heartfelt promise to visit their little vineyard the next time I was in the region, as they'd invited me to do. Walking back to the car, I made a private vow to save the gift bottle to share with Jane and several friends when I returned home.

The winding, traffic-free drive back down the scenic valley lent itself to the cocoon of quiet thought the encounter had spun. Pulling off once more at a scenic overlook near the river, I sat gazing out at a small vineyard, reflecting. That French viniculture was *en crise* hadn't surprised me, in light of such hard international realities as those illuminated by *Mondovino* and the country's general economic malaise. I knew that barely more than one percent of France's population remained on the farm, a percentage that continued to shrink even as the size of the surviving farms grew larger. The numbers were sadly similar to those in America, though the size of the average farm in France—90% of them remained under 600 acres—would have been considered miniscule in the United States. By any measure, the Dols' multi-cropped 150-acre holding was of a size that imperiled the family's centuries-old heritage of tilling its chalky soil to *gagner sa vie*. Clearly, for all its quaint charm, a village market held on a winter Sunday spoke of the same gritty endurance people had always needed to make a life as small farmers, whether here or on the American prairie. It was as out of touch with reality to romanticize their work as it was the twelve-hour workdays my father had sweated in a sandhills hayfield, or the fact my mother had given birth to me on the kitchen table, the nearest hospital being thirty miles away.

I pulled back onto the road and drove on, trying to fit a rural world that felt more anachronistic with every passing year into the tangled complexities of the present. One of the most impenetrable was the tariff and farm subsidy clash that within the past few years had pitted nation against nation, and most recently, nearly all of them against France.

Perspective on the key issues was hard to come by. For every balanced analysis there seemed to be a dozen publicizing the extremes—the fact that a Prince Albert of Monaco could receive half a million dollars in annual subsidies, for example, versus the counter-claim that reducing support payments to farmers would kill the French way of life. The critics, nearly all of them non-French, demonstrably had some compelling evidence to buttress their claim that tariffs harmed developing countries and that subsidies were both unfairly distributed and similarly trade-distorting: 80% of the payments went to 20% of the farmers; wheat, beef, and milk were heavily subsidized while fruits, vegetables, pigs, and poultry were not; Chirac's refusal to bend on the issue had seriously strained relationships both abroad and within the E.U.

But the opposition, to my eye at least, made a case no less strong. I hadn't asked the Dols if they received subsidies, but I had no more doubt of the *terroir*'s dependence on them than I had of my Nebraska friend Ed's judgment when I'd asked him how the fifty cents he received for each bushel of his corn would impact his life if it were lost. "If they pull all the subsidies," he'd answered, "it would be a disaster for a lot of us in this state." I knew too that E.U. reforms adopted in 2003 would eventually convert the bulk of the bloc's production subsidies into less trade-distorting programs such as animal-welfare and environmental-management grants to farmers, and that French public support of tariffs, even those that made their *fromage* and *bœuf bourgignon* significantly more expensive, was grounded in trust of the quality they were paying for and a fear of the more industrial, chemically juiced food imported from abroad.

All of it helped explain the nation's stubborn resistance to outside pressure. But there was perhaps one thing more—a far less cerebral reason that retained the visceral power of what ran deepest through the collective unconscious. I had seen it alluded to in a perceptive analysis of the subsidy dispute in the *Financial Times*, but glimpsed it more directly during my interview with the septuagenarian Marots in Arromanches—their description of the Nazi Occupation and the severe "privations" in the cities, the fact that in the campagne, there was always food.

However baffling and out of touch it might seem to others, in short, the French's reverence for the *terroir* marked an attitude that ran deep in my own bloodstream. Biased or not, they showed an admirable willingness to sacrifice the material allure of cheaper, environmentally insidious foods for the more expensive varieties protected under specific "Geographic Indications"—the increasing array of items from wine and cheese to yellow-legged chickens that gave the nation its incomparably rich bounty of regional *terroirs*. How many small family-owned farms might have survived in America, I wondered in comparison, if we'd been equally inclined to look past price tags to the quality, taste, and preservation of traditional values that couldn't be tallied on the bottom line? I drove on past the narrow valley's scattered little plots and vineyards thinking of the classic final line of Voltaire's *Candide*, "But we must cultivate our gardens." In the eighteenth century, "*jardins*" had meant both gardens and fields.

"*Malheureusement*," her *Logis* was closed during the week, the owner had regretfully informed me at breakfast when I'd impulsively tried to book a second night in the snug little room above the trout stream. During the winter she took guests only on weekends. But *heureusement*, at least from where I was sitting, she'd quickly recommended another overlooking the larger river back in Cahors, then graciously volunteered to phone the hotel and make a reservation in my name. Relieved, I headed back to the walled town warmed by the country kindness and generosity I'd been shown.

Running low on gas, I circled the Cahors *périphérique* searching for a station, chastising myself for not having filled the car the day before. It had long ago ceased to be something you thought about in America, but finding a place open in *la France profonde* on a Sunday was still far from a sure thing. Eventually sighting an occupied pump by a supermarket, I pulled in. The middle-aged woman filling her own Peugeot was the only person there. The *caisse* booth was locked and empty. I inserted the nozzle from the pump beside hers knowing it was going to be my credit card or nothing on this winter afternoon.

Since I'd always paid with cash at European gas stations, the next step was terra incognita, and after several failed attempts at getting the card to work I shuffled abashedly over to the Frenchwoman to see how it was done. She patiently explained the process to me, then reappeared at my side after finishing her own fill when it became apparent I still hadn't figured the system out. Taking the card from my hand, she couldn't get it to work either, another of the week's several pointed reminders of Aldo Leopold's pithy axiom. I still didn't have any gas, but my shriveled male ego had at least not taken another hit. Minutes later, the two of us finally got the job done through a kind of makeshift, cross-cultural collaboration: I gave the woman a fifty-euro bill, and pumped the gas using her card. Returning it, I thanked her fervently for being so helpful, and asked if she knew of a hotel called *La Chartreuse*. "*Oui*," she answered, smiling, and before I could voice a polite word of protest she turned back to her own car with a cheerful "*suivez-moi*"—follow me.

I'll never know whether the several kilometers I trailed her along the river also led toward her own destination, but this further example of French graciousness to an American stranger so soon after the Dols' *cadeau* filled me with gratitude whatever the case. A few hundred yards after we'd passed the old medieval bridge, she pulled up at the hotel entrance, pausing just long enough for another "*de rien*" wave out her window before driving on. It's unlikely she caught the belated tip of my cap in her rearview mirror—saw the "*Chapeau, Madame*" on my lips as her car vanished up the street.

That night, for the first time since leaving Paris, I switched on the television set in my room to check the news. The womb-like oblivion from the world's turbulence was one of the quiet pleasures I'd always found in foreign travel, but something had happened not long after I checked into the attractive hotel that had pricked my curiosity. Out on a late afternoon exercise run, I had happened on a private tennis club, and as I stood outside the office, waiting to speak with the occupied pro in the hope of arranging an hour lesson, a Frenchman walking his dog approached from up the street. Pausing beside me while the roving Lab left its calling card on several nearby bushes, the man seemed as disposed to time-killing conversation as I was, and we were soon involved in a surprisingly spirited exchange. It was clear from the outset that he spoke English fairly well, but his demeanor was stiff and prickly enough I persisted for some time in French, before finally surrendering to his obvious pride at being able to harangue me in my native tongue.

The man was roughly my own age, coppery-haired and goateed, and it took him only a few moments to raise the subject of politics—specifically the man whose re-election had spurred my trip. I hadn't told him where I was from, but he homed in with a bloodhound's nose for the spoor. "Your great President," he said with biting sarcasm, "is right now in Brussels. He makes a brilliant speech last night." Unsure how much of the scorn was directed at me, simply as an American, I told him I had worked for the opposition candidate. "Of course," he said, looking dubious, "but over fifty percent of your countrymen voted for Bush." The election's result had shocked people in France, he went on. They had thought Kerry would surely win.

He was into the subject with so much feeling I let him roll on unchecked. It was all "because of religion" he declared acidly, turning briefly away to call his dog back from a foray onto the red clay of a nearby court. "The best thing we ever did in France was to separate the church from the government," he turned back to me, peering hard into my face. He repeated the point for emphasis. "The people who elect your President live in fear," he continued with a mirthless laugh. "They are the same as the ones you are fighting—the Musulman terrorists." My government was dangerous, he shook his head contemptuously, a threat to the world.

The club pro emerged at that point, agreeing readily to the

requested lesson, and I spent the next hour taking out some of the conflicted emotions the diatribe had stirred in me on an onslaught of tennis balls aimed at my incorrigibly weak backhand. But what the acerbic Frenchman had said about the speech in Brussels continued to fester, and I made a mental note to follow up on it that night back in my room.

What had long struck me as an American tuning into the public airwaves of France, compared to the programming back home, was the relative absence of commercials and of shows aimed at our basest human instincts. While the level of what the French colloquially dubbed la *télé poubelle*—trash t.v.—was clearly rising as stations ran more confessional talk-shows and French spin-offs of American reality series, any objective traveler from the States channel-surfing a hotel room's set for even a short time felt the difference. It was no surprise to learn that the maximum amount of permissible advertising per hour was twelve minutes, that the overall average was around seven, and that films and children's programs could be interrupted no more than once every thirty-five minutes for ads.

The hotels I stayed in on the trip typically carried between six and ten channels. Most of those ran primarily news and talk programs, movies, soccer matches, game shows, and—again by comparison with America—a startling number of long, PBS-style documentaries on an unlimited range of topics from around the world. Nearly all were uninterrupted by ads, which appeared in a sequential block between programs introduced with the advisory word "*Publicité*," colloquially shortened to "*La Pub*." The movies and serials, often dubbed or subtitled, showed more explicit sex but significantly less graphic violence. Drama series were decidedly middle-brow, including dubbed reruns of *Law & Order* and *N.Y.P.D. Blue*. (No TV experience I've ever had quite compares with hearing Andy Sipowicz shout "*Je vous ai dit pour la dernière fois, asseyez-vous!*")

I had little doubt the President's appearance in Brussels that had so exercised my dog-walking acquaintance would be featured on that night's news, and I hoped to catch what I could of it to draw my own conclusions. Waiting for it, I lay on the bed idly switching channels, eventually holding on a Swedish-made documentary which appeared to deal with an Iranian father's frustrated attempts to contact his long-lost daughter in the United States. The father's English was heavily accented but fluent. Though I'd missed the program's beginning, the main lines of the story soon began to emerge.

The Iranian was a physician who three decades earlier had lived in Michigan, where he'd married and developed a thriving practice, eventually buying a beautiful lakefront home. A child, the now-grownup woman he sought, was born. Somehow, for reasons I hadn't tuned in the program early enough to learn, he had ended up back in Tehran without a passport, where he'd been forced to remain for many years.

The documentary flowed on with little external commentary, the viewer left to draw his or her own conclusions from the revealing faces and voices, but slowly the subtler facets of the story also began to clear. Not long after the physician arrived in Tehran, his wife had filed for divorce, and the Michigan court, ostensibly because he couldn't be located, had awarded her everything they'd jointly possessed: the new house, all its contents, and the only thing that now mattered to him, full custody of the child. No paternal visitation rights had been granted. The old man on the screen shook his head in quiet anguish. The same American court system that supposedly had been unable to locate him when he might still have found legal representation, he lamented, had somehow managed to mail the judge's final decree to his Tehran address a week after the judgment was made.

Seconds later I found myself staring at the screen, like unknown numbers of other viewers throughout France, sizing up a portly American judge seated in his Michigan office, his hearty Midwestern voice flowing familiarly into my room. The off-camera reporter asked if the court's decision in the Dr. Mahmoud case could have had anything to do with the era's political realities—the fact that it had happened during the Carter administration's hostage crisis in Iran. "Absolutely not!" the judge responded with feeling. "You can be totally sure any Iranian in this courtroom would have been given the red carpet treatment. This is a country of law." But what about the consequences of the decision, the Swedish reporter followed up, polite but persistent. Everything Dr. Mahmoud had was taken from him—his child, his home, even his private papers and books. "I wasn't aware of that," the judge answered evenly. "No one could reach him. Anyway, all that's water under the bridge now, '*a fate ohcomplay*.' But I'm sure you understand that," he added, smirking. "You're from over there."

He was the kind of man I'd known all my life, might even have felt some brief kinship with in different circumstances, sitting next to him in a football stadium or a duck blind. A hail-fellow good old boy from the American heartland who wasn't being consciously dishonest—truly might have rolled out his red carpet for the more palatable foreigners who appeared in his court. But I knew he was also a man unlikely to be troubled by Abu Ghraib or Guantanamo or almost any other course of action our country took in the name of freedom, and I was thus unsurprised, though sickened, by what he said next.

"Don't you think Dr. Mahmoud was treated unjustly," the reporter pressed quietly on, "looking back now at the evidence—the facts about his situation the court apparently didn't have then?"

The judge leaned toward the camera and his voice took on a steely edge it had lacked previously, the voice of the überpatriot General Ripper in *Dr. Strangelove*. "If I was the government," he said, "I'd bomb all of them. I mean that. You can't trust these people. They're fanatics. They don't understand the meaning of law or liberty. We need to teach 'em a lesson. And I'll tell ya one thing more—you'd only have to do it once. That's all it would take. We're way too tolerant of 'em. Once is all it would take."

It was all I could take, the Souillac youth's '*vulgar*' burned into my soul like a brand, but I forced myself to watch the program to its painful end. The concluding scenes showed the old man trying to telephone his now-grown daughter, whose number he'd managed to locate after years of separation. As I continued to sit in the darkened hotel room, watching, I couldn't shake the thought of all those French viewers watching with me, the impressions being formed of my country in the wake of recent events. I envisioned the hat-tipping old Maquis veteran who had bought me the complimentary drink, fired by a half-century of respect for America and Americans—the sharp-eyed, skeptical Alex watching with Yann in Souillac, perhaps sharing a repellant thought or two about *"l'autre homme du Michigan"*—*wasn't that the state he also said he was from?*—who had pressed them with so many pointed questions two days before. Together, we hear the daughter pick up the phone and answer, the father identify himself — the interminable pause before she says curtly "No one by that name lives here" as the phone abruptly goes dead at his ear. Undeterred, the old man calls many more times over the ensuing weeks but now she neither answers nor responds to his recorded messages. Ultimately, using the Iranian passport he's finally been granted, he flies to Helsinki and writes a letter to the American Embassy. After waiting several days to be sure it has arrived, he makes his last desperate appeal.

We never see the young woman at the other end of the phone line, only hear her voice as the camera holds on the physician's careworn face. "There's nothing we can do for you," the voice says with finality. "You don't have a green card. And I don't have any authority to act. I must also tell you that, if you do try to enter the United States, you'll be arrested. You need to understand that, and I want to be clear."

"I do understand that," the old man says stoically. "I don't want to work there. I only want to see my daughter. I thought perhaps... simply as a gesture of humanity... you might be able to do something to make that possible. I'll meet her anywhere," he adds, pleading, "wherever she wants."

"No," the bodiless voice repeats once more, "I have no authority to do anything about that. I'm sorry. But I have to tell you again— you'll be arrested if you try to enter the United States."

The documentary concluded with Dr. Mahmoud's response as this last hope went up in smoke and still another phone clicked off in his ear. For several moments he remained silent, this final verdict registering like a death sentence on his weary face. When words came they were barely audible, the voice of quiet resignation and bottomless grief. "No, I don't blame them," he whispered. "Everyone did what they could…. There was nothing anyone could do."

The news came on a short time later. As the dog-walking Frenchman had promised, my President's visit to the Belgian city which served as headquarters of both NATO and the European Union was the lead story. Self-assured and smiling, Mr. Bush stood regally under a crystal chandelier in a high-ceilinged room framed with blood-red drapes and paintings of royalty. Yet his message, complete with the Texas twang and dropped g's that had served him so well through four years of governance and a successful re-election, might have been recorded in Amarillo or Dubuque. Russia must make a commitment to the rule of law, he warned near the beginning. "May God bless you all," he closed. Most of what came in between was larded with frequent repetitions of the words "freedom" and "liberty." Numerous hints dropped by White House officials prior to the speech that a major emphasis would be on American "partnership" with the E.U. had proved meaningless, the newscaster reported. Journalists had been kept behind velvet ropes at the rear of the room, hundreds of protesters held at bay outside the hall. Tired beyond words, I switched off the set and fell asleep.

The next morning, I crossed the river on the modern bridge near the hotel and walked the half-mile back down the opposite shoreline to the Pont Valentré, built at the beginning of a century-long war that had finally petered out in an inconclusive stasis, both sides exhausted by the endless drain of money and blood. I stood there a long time, staring at it. The slits in the stonework where French archers had rained arrows down on their mortal enemy were now only picturesque openings on the snow-fringed cliffs in the distance, the grim watchtowers mere stone sentinels in the photo albums of visitors from abroad. Pulling my jacket tighter against a freshening wind, I walked on under the crennelated arch and crossed over, returned to the hotel on the empty road the genial Frenchwoman had led me down the day before.

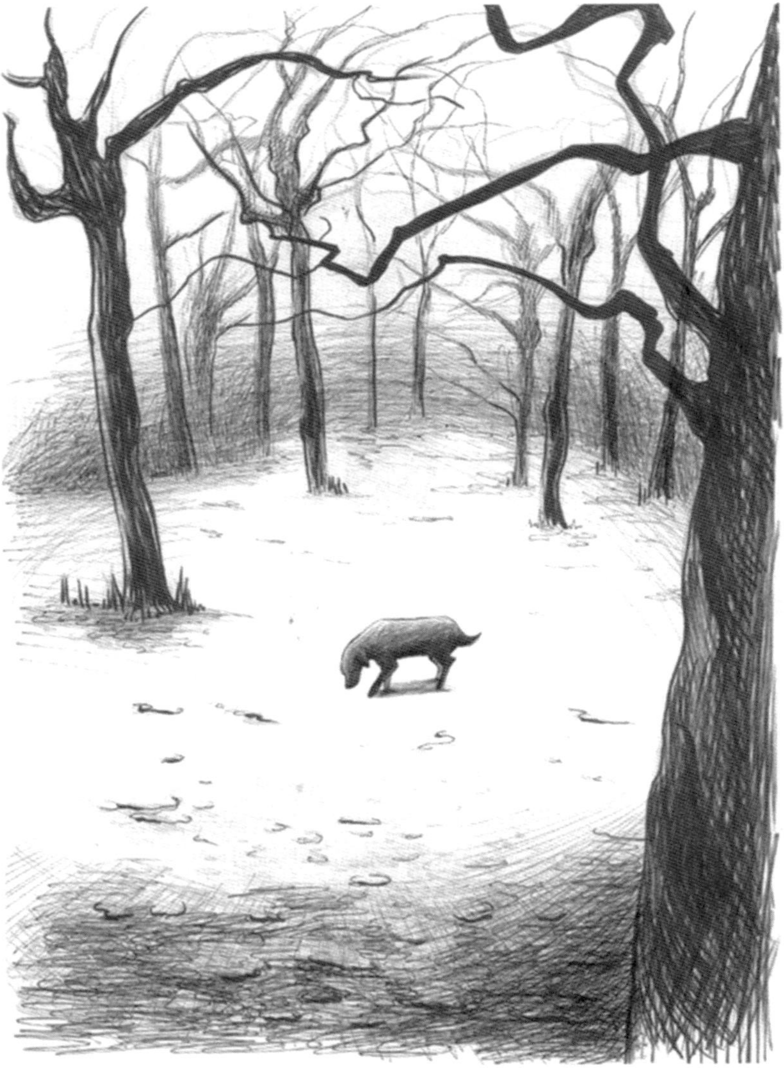

Chapter 6
Margot

"No, monsieur," the young woman bent closer, her voice dropping to a conspiratorial whisper. "They are *conservées*. If you want the *fraîches* ones—they are the best in the world—you must go to *Lalbenque*. It is not far away."

Her name was Estelle. In my three nights at L'Hôtel Chartreuse, she had been my waiter, a transplanted Parisian with piercing eyes and close-cropped auburn hair who had settled in Cahors for much the same reason the young people I'd met in Souillac had remained there. She loved the region's wild beauty, she told me as I dawdled over a *profiterole* the first night, the slower pace of life in the Quercy and its down-to-earth allure. We'd exchanged other bits of personal background and perspective the next evening. But on this, my last night in the pleasant dining room overlooking the river, I'd chosen an entrée that sent a shiver of excitement through me the moment I noticed it on the *carte*, a choice she clearly considered a grave error.

Treasure hunts had always fascinated me. The mystique of *Treasure Island* ranked with Tom and Huck's discovery of the gold in Injun Joe's cave on my scale of most indelible childhood bedtime stories. Back then, Easter had been my favorite holiday, surpassing even the gift-bonanza of Christmas, for the egg hunts my parents took a fiendish delight in making as challenging as they could. I never ate the eggs. What thrilled me was the adrenaline rush of the hunt—that matchless moment when an overturned leaf or rotting gunny sack yielded a brightly painted egg on the spring-green lawn.

It was that starry-eyed love of the quest that the aptly-named Estelle's whispered words had stirred in me. The world held all kinds of treasures, from the impossibly extravagant to those that didn't cost a penny, and over half a century of pursuing game and fish and backstreet flamenco hideaways I'd chased too many of them to count. Checking out of the hotel the next morning, I could see Jane in my mind's eye rolling her eyes and saying "There he goes again." But the promised village lay only thirty kilometers distant. And another hotel employee had confirmed the waiter's directive—go to Lalbenque if you want *les truffes*.

Truffles. For decades, somewhere back near the dawn of my infatuation with France, what seemed near-mystical tales about the subterranean fungi had captivated me. They were supposedly worth their weight in gold. Smelled and tasted like the mythic ambrosia. Were rooted up by super-intelligent pigs in secret haunts thieves would kill to know. Studying the *carte* that last evening in the Cahors hotel, after two nights of happily settling for the more economical *menu*, I was helplessly hooked the instant my eyes fell on the words "*Nos spécialités autour de la truffe.*" I had no idea what the *spécialités* were. That they had *truffes* in them was all I cared about.

Estelle's frowning shake of the head had managed to dissuade me, barely, but it wasn't until I arrived at the tiny village whose enticing name she'd whispered that I realized she had sent me to the French mecca of *trufficulture*. The sign at the edge of town read "*Centre Principal De Production Des TRUFFES Noires du Quercy.*" The main street was labeled "*Rue du Marché aux Truffes.*" And it wasn't mere civic hype. Every Tuesday, buyers came from all over France, and beyond, to negotiate with the locals in an afternoon market where the prices sometimes reached seven hundred euros a kilo—close to a thousand dollars for two pounds of fungus. Unfortunately, I'd rolled down the empty *Rue du Marché* on a Thursday. The experience of watching agents from Paris haggle the price of the next Maxim's or Tour d'Argent's gourmet blowout would have to wait for another trip. If Jane had been with me, I would probably have bent to her eye-rolling common sense and driven on, however dispiritedly. But that voice of reason remained an ocean away, and the *truffe* tide was running full. The only doubt I had in those giddy moments was how to plunge in.

The challenge was daunting. I didn't know a soul in the town, had no idea which of the small farms I'd passed on the road through the wooded hills winding up to it might harbor a truffle hunter. And finding such a person was not going to help much in any case. For by that point (a realization that dawned only after I'd reached the village) merely tasting a fresh truffle—even the best truffle in the world—was a secondary objective. I wanted more. Ridiculously more. Something I couldn't yet fully acknowledge even to myself.

I drove slowly on down the *Rue du Marché,* hoping for some sudden inspiration or stroke of luck like those I'd had in Arromanches and Souillac. Accosting a native on the street and blurting "*Excusez-moi, Monsieur, je cherche quelqu'un qui cherche les trufffes*" wasn't out of the question, but only as a last resort. It occurred to me that this was what turned people into obsessive treasure hunters—the kick that came when a mud-choked sunken hulk turned out to be a gold-hauling galleon, or some obscure, brush-covered hole in the ground opened out into a majestic cave. Or was the thrill simply the hunt itself, the will-sapping obstacles, regardless of the end?

A few months earlier, I'd had a long night's discussion of the subject with a close friend I'd known since childhood, our relationship having survived almost half a century of geographical and psychological distance that had left us gazing out at the mysteries of life from opposite poles. The fact was more pronounced because our lives had begun in eerily similar places. We were within a few weeks of being the same age. His first name, Bruce, was the same as mine on our birth certificates. Our parents had been married in 1940 on the same June afternoon. Inevitably, we grew up playing sports against each other—our mirror-image towns of 450 people were less than fifteen miles apart—then went on to the same small Lutheran college where we quickly became roommates. Yet after graduation our paths had diverged just as quickly, to the point where Bruce remained a devout church-goer and equally devoted Republican as well as several other things I'd once been but had drifted away from decades before.

Somehow, none of the psychic distance mattered much when we were together, as we'd recently come to be for an annual spring fishing trip after many years of only sporadic Christmas-card contact. You make the same look-the-other-way exceptions for the friends of your youth that you do for house pets and ne'er-do-well uncles, a fact the other's perceived political sins had forced Bruce and I to confirm every time we met. The counter-balance, at least in my case, was that whenever we got together we fell back almost at once into the bantering familiarity of our student days. He remained what he had always been—eccentric, but reflexively kind and decent. I found his politics incomprehensible, but knew they held none of the jingoistic venom of the smug judge I'd found so repellent in the television documentary, the arrogant hypocrisies of the Washington neocons.

My friend came to mind as I sat parked at the end of the *Rue de Marché aux Truffes* because he was the one person I knew who at that moment would have understood—have *felt*—what I was feeling. He might never have heard of truffles, but I'd seen his eyes take on the crazed gleam of a Captain Ahab too many times to count. The sketchiest rumor of some remote, impossibly fertile trout pool was enough to bring out the fever in his soul.

I decided to pursue a solution to my dilemma at a little *charcuterie* I'd passed just up the street. Waiting outside for a pair of customers to clear, I killed time reading the labels of pâte tins in the window, then bucked up my resolve and entered the shop when the busy woman behind the counter appeared briefly unoccupied. Pointing to the pâtes, I asked for her advice on the tastiest of them. Hastily buying the half dozen she recommended, I pointed to a much tinier container I'd noticed on the shelf behind her, no larger than an aspirin bottle but labeled with the magic word, *truffe*. "Oui," she nodded, plucking it down with her fingertips and handing it to me. The price on the lid read thirty-five euros. It would have flushed close to fifty dollars out of my travel funds.

Still, thinking a scrutiny of its label might inch me closer to the grail, I was on the verge of buying it too, but the smiling shopkeeper showed the same grace that prevents most people from taking advantage of drunks and children. Five minutes later, I stood holding an even more miniscule jar and watching her animated demonstration, complete with a gleaming saucepan retrieved from the back room, of how to prepare an omelette with the single truffle my fifteen euros had bought. Tucking the precious fungus away like a sacred bone enshrined in a reliquary, I tested the woman's indulgence further—asked for something that, *dommage,* couldn't be found in even such a delightful establishment as hers.

It was the iffiest plea for aid I'd made in a trip already filled with them. But the woman didn't bat an eye. "*Oui,*" she said, misunderstanding my stumbling French, it might still be possible for me to see a *truffe fraîche* even though market day had passed two days earlier. A vendor lived a few kilometers away, in a neighboring village. "Monsieur Jouglas," she enunciated his name, taking obvious pains that I not misconstrue it. If anyone could help me, Monsieur Jouglas was the one.

One baby-step leads to another, I told myself, returning to the car and stowing this latest bag of impulsive purchases under the seat. A half hour later I rolled through the gates of *Le Colombier,* past a sign neatly lettered "*M. Jouglas et Fils.*" A man in his mid-thirties I took to be the son emerged from the barn a minute later, and after a formal greeting, did his patient best to answer the string of increasingly muddled questions I posed. Not since Arromanches had the foreign language curse struck as virulently—a Frenchman's speech that left my brain spinning like a rudderless boat swept down a set of rapids at breakneck speed. I kept asking, the farmer kept answering, until finally some chance combination of words and gestures got through. Nodding bemusedly, he led me to the dead-bolted door of a dark, low-roofed building a few yards past his office. Unlocking it, he beckoned me inside and switched on a light. And there, at last, was what I had come to see.

I'll put the next sentence as delicately as I can. If you were driving down a country road in France and happened on a thousand-dollar pile of truffles that had just fallen from a *trufficulteur*'s panel truck, you'd swerve to the side and avert your nose. For they look exactly like a fresh dropping of turds. Black. Ill-shapen. The kind of ubiquitous stain on the sidewalks of Paris that's made the City of Light a nerve-wracking mine field Jane tiptoes through like a thief in the night. The farmer plucked one of the larger ones out of the wooden box and ceremoniously handed it to me. I felt its tight-grained heft. Turned it over in my palm. Lifted it to my nostrils and smiled in that forced, self-conscious way you smile when a sommelier pours a splash of wine into your glass and stands stiffly waiting for your response to its bouquet. The fungus's delicate odor was surprisingly faint, far less pronounced than I expected, though I'd been assured by Madame, back in the *charcuterie*, that stirred into an omelette, then refrigerated for two days in a sealed container, the morsel I'd bought would explode in aromatic bliss. And who was I to doubt her? I remembered a story I'd read of the dying *Chef d'État* Mitterand, whose last requested meal was a tiny, illegally-killed wild bird called an *ortolan*. Prepared in the timeless French tradition, entrails intact, after days of soaking in a bath of Armagnac, the exotic bird was served to the enfeebled President on his deathbed, a towel draped over his head lest even the faintest of its ambrosial odors escape his olfactory glands. However deep my francophilia, the story served as a reminder that a few places remained where I hoped I'd never go.

My obsession with *les truffes*, on the other hand, had only been whetted by finally touching and smelling one. Groping for the words in French, I blurted to Monsieur Jouglas what I hadn't confessed to the woman in the *charcuterie*: could I have a look at the gifted pig that had found them? Snout, stump, or whiskered nostril, I was keen to see the superporcine nose.

The farmer's brow furrowed, and it was instantly apparent I had pushed the envelope too far. "*Pas un porc*," he muttered. "*Un chien.*" That much of his French I caught. Truffles were hunted with dogs, not pigs. I also grasped that he hadn't personally found the ones he'd been kind enough to show me. Switching off the light, he led me back out into the farmyard. It was depressingly clear I would find no *truffe*-hunting animal at *Le Colombier*. Still, I wanted to thank him as best I could for the pains he'd taken to indulge me. The farm had a small salesroom, and five minutes later I walked out holding still another bag to stash under the car seat, this one containing a tin of foie-gras and a second truffle in a walnut-size jar. My wallet was getting thinner with every stop, but that homecoming omelette was taking on a three-star Michelin cachet.

Walking me back to the car, the farmer suddenly grunted a cryptic "*moment*" and stepped into his cluttered office. Through the dusty window I could see him paging through a phone book, and a moment later he returned with a slip of paper in his hand. "*Monsieur Vincens*," he said, pointing to the scribbled name and a phone number. "*Peut-être....*" A few indecipherable words followed, and he saw me off with that inscrutable Gallic shrug.

I drove back down the *Rue de Marché* a half-hour later, searching now simply for a telephone, on what had taken on the unmistakable feel of a wild goose chase. The single booth I eventually found took only phone cards, and not having one, I walked on up the street to a small grocery and asked the owner if he had any for sale. He shook his head no. Was there another booth in the village that took coins? No, he said—who do you wish to call? I showed him the slip of paper the farmer had given me. Nodding, he picked up his cell phone and dialed the number, then handed the phone to me. The voice that answered was aloof, crisp as a December morning, the voice of a man who didn't suffer fools gladly. The upside was that I could understand nearly every word he spoke. As the store owner watched with amused interest, I pressed on.

"Monsieur Jouglas was kind enough to give me your name, monsieur," I explained in the most deferential French I could muster. "He told me you were the most knowledgeable authority in the Quercy on *les truffes*."

The clipped response remained guarded, but sounded slightly less wintry. I glanced again at the slyly grinning storekeeper, who nodded when I pointed to the rear of the store and lifted my eyebrows in a silent plea to continue the conversation there. Slavishly grateful for the privacy, I took awkward refuge behind a row of cereal boxes and resumed the diplomatic overture to the disembodied voice at the other end of the line. I was an American, I said (as if it weren't obvious) and had long been fascinated by truffle hunting. Was there any possibility I could talk with him about how it was done? Several seconds of dead silence followed, then the gruff clearing of a throat, the line stilled again for several seconds more. Finally the cool Gallic voice responded. *Oui*, it might be possible. He was driving into town at *quatorze heures*, the Frenchman said stiffly. He would meet me on the sidewalk in front of *la mairie*.

When the phone clicked off, I felt like I'd arranged an audience with the Pope, and that was before the chuckling storekeeper informed me that Monsieur Vincens was "*Le Président*" of the region's "*Syndicat des Trufficulteurs.*" The news was daunting enough I spent the next hour working up another list of written questions like those I'd scribbled before my interview in the Irish pub a few days before. In what I hoped was a well-omened coincidence, *Le Président*'s first name also happened to be Jean-Paul, the same as the Souillac wine merchant's. Yet this second set of queries proved far more difficult to write. The first few dealt merely with truffles and truffle-hunting—the kind of information I could no doubt have easily gotten in ten minutes back home on the Internet. The difficulty, I finally had to admit to myself, wasn't the formidable voice of French officialdom I'd heard on the telephone, or even the likelihood of coming off as a slack-jawed *plouc*. It was the wall I hit whenever I considered ways of phrasing what I *actually* wanted to ask him. For pleased as I would be to learn the mysteries of his arcane craft, or even more, to meet his truffle-hunting porker or canine, what I really wanted was to *hunt* with him—to experience the thrill of the quest. And given the guy's glacial diffidence, that prospect seemed about as likely as Bush and Chirac hunkering down in a bass boat to hash out their differences over a six-pack of beer.

Nibbling on a bread crust spread with one of the pâtes I'd bought from the *charcuterie* woman, I considered further the roots of this latest personal obsession. Why a trifle like *truffles*, of all things? It couldn't simply be their exotic reputation, or the hurdles one had to jump even for the remote chance of trailing an animal through the woods in the faint hope of discovering one. Several minutes passed as I sat in the silent car, reflecting, before a realization struck with something like the emotional force of Proust's madeleine. The delectable food I was distractedly nibbling might even have triggered it. For the answer lay in the *mushroom*—not the French fungus but the memories that clung to another nearly as prized that grew in my own wooded part of America. *The morel.* When its brain-tissuey image came to me, I knew at once it was what explained the spell I'd been under since Estelle's whispered words fell on my ear.

Morels weren't truffles, in either gourmet price or exotic reputation. But they were rare and valuable enough to draw legions of devotees into the Minnesota woods on secretive searches every spring. You could set your clock by their annual appearance. They would pop out of the ground, most often in the neighborhood of dying elm trees, when the first lilacs bloomed in the dooryard. And in years with a shortage of rain, they could become almost as precious as the fabled *truffes* of France.

I had hunted them from the first year I lived in Minnesota—spent a few days every spring thinking of little else but my private treasure haunts. The wonderful taste and aroma of fresh morels sauteed in butter was almost enough to warrant a towel draped over the head. And they were even better mixed into an omelette, the further realization came to me. The *charcuterie* lady had simply shown me a different technique.

Such associations alone might have explained the truffle obsession. But there was one more, and I knew beyond doubt it was what lay beneath them all. Almost twenty years earlier, when my youngest son was a sixth-grader, his mother and I had divorced and he'd moved with her to St. Paul, a hundred miles away. Though I made frequent trips up to visit him throughout the subsequent years of his adolescence, the pain of his absence was always present. Occasionally, Andy would take the three-hour bus ride back down the Mississippi River road after he finished school on Friday, and we'd have two uninterrupted days to spend together. In the springtime, unfailingly, that meant trout fishing and searching for morels.

At first, back when the ritual was born, not long after my son was out of diapers, I'd walk past an obscure bed of the mushrooms and slowly circle it in silence until I heard his delighted cry. Later, he needed no such paternal indulgence, but his delight remained as intense as my own. Waiting in that little French village for my tight-lipped host, a man so distant my phone call might have reached him on Olympus, I remembered those vanished days with a wash of nostalgia stronger than any I'd felt for some time.

Le Président appeared in the flesh fifteen minutes after the hour he'd appointed—a slight, wiry man with shrewd eyes and a regal flow of snowy hair. A pronounced stoop I attributed to several decades of probing the earth for *truffes* marked his posture. Shaking hands, I thanked him for agreeing to meet with me, then asked if I could buy him a glass of wine or cup of coffee at the café just up the street. No, he said, he'd just had *le déjeuner*. He led me instead into the *mairie*, and our interview began.

Throughout my prepared list of questions he remained unfailingly attentive, but the dialogue had a palpably more journalistic feel than my experience in the Souillac pub. Nor was there any of the easy bonhomie I'd experienced with the Dols in the St. Géry market. *Vraiment,* he said, the local mushrooms were special. Truffles came in several species, yes, that was true as well, but the most gastronomically valued and expensive was "*la truffe noire*" that grew in the Quercy woods at the base of young oaks. *Non*, pigs weren't much used anymore. Dogs were easier to train and more mobile. *Oui*, he bowed his head with patrician humility, he and his dogs had been very successful. Seven years earlier, on a career-day, they had found ten kilos in a single afternoon.

Imagining such a treasure trove brought a palpable frisson to my flesh, and I asked if he got one too, after so many years of collecting them, at the moment the dog struck the scent. He peered deep into my eyes before answering. *Oui*, he said softly, especially when it came in a place he had never before found them. Whenever that happened, "*absolument, le frisson.*"

It certainly remained there for me, however vicariously, listening to him describe it. But even as his hands fluttered delicately over his stomach to illustrate, his voice kept its quiet reserve. I had reached the end of my written list and couldn't think of anything else to ask him—only the last, burning question I'd tamped down all day. The words tightening in my throat, I began to blurt it—"*Est-ce qu'il y a une possibilité de…?*" —then ran abruptly aground on the shoals of cowardice. Or maybe it was simply a momentary dose of common sense. Even without Jane there to restrain me, it was too much to ask. Defeated, I bit back the words and asked him only if there was any possibility I could snap a photo of his dog.

The letdown was so acute it didn't remotely occur to me at the time that even this request was more than a little eccentric, a fact that registered only when I saw the expression it brought to the Frenchman's face. To say he looked surprised would be an understatement. Shocked would be too strong. The look was more like that of a man who'd glanced down and discovered his new puppy had just peed on his shoes. Before he could express whatever he was feeling, I forged on. I hunted them myself, I blurted—*les champignons*—back in America. Fungus fascinated me. Fungus was addictive. Fungus was as good as it got. The *paysage* around my home even resembled Quercy, I lurched to an end, though we didn't have any *truffes*.

What part of America, he asked, appearing faintly interested, though it might simply have been relief that I seemed to have dropped the idea of photographing his dog. "Minnesota...the upper Mississippi River valley," I answered. Every spring I headed for the woods in search of *les morilles*.

The words touched the place I'd given up on finding in him, as if they'd lit a match behind his eyes. "*Les morilles!*" he repeated passionately, he searched for them too—preferred them even to *truffes* if they were prepared well! With the suddenness of a change in the weather, the two of us were no longer journalist and interviewee but a pair of aging men sharing the timeless excitement of a quest we both loved. He asked me where I found most of my mushrooms and I told him under dying trees, the French word for *elms* escaping me. He nodded sagely, and for the next several minutes we exchanged other bits of information as the light continued to shine in his eyes.

It was then quite close to three o'clock in the afternoon. The President of the truffle society in France's truffle center had taken half an hour out of his day to meet with a pushy American stranger. What he said next is something I hope I'll remember the next time I hear one of my countrymen trash "the Frogs." "Meet me back here at *quinze heures quinze*," he gestured crisply to the wall clock. "I have some business I must take care of, but I will be finished then."

An hour later I was back on the road again, trailing his white panel truck up a narrow, winding route through the oak-covered countryside. A few kilometers farther on he pulled into a lane and stopped to unlock a barred metal gate. His house lay just beyond it, a shuttered two-story building with a well-built kennel at its side. Three nondescript dogs yapped and jumped excitedly as we approached.

Opening the woven-wire door slightly, *Le Président* let the largest squeeze out, using his body as a barrier to keep the other two pressing behind from following. To my eye, the chosen one was an undersized, half-breed black Lab, but the Frenchman said nothing to introduce us. Whatever its parentage, I had my truffle-hunting dog at last, and reached for the disposable camera in my pocket to snap the picture I'd so brazenly pressed to take. But my taciturn guide walked on, back toward his house, the dog scampering ahead as I trailed both of them bewilderedly. "*Margot!*" he shouted at the hopped-up animal. "*Margot—ici!*" We moved on, past the stone house, down a snow-fringed lane into a thin stand of lichen-covered oak trees. Yes, I thought, this is much better—a picture of the dog in the woods, not simply perched domestically outside its kennel door. The dog was snuffling around in the leaves, her feet pawing the ground, and I quickly pulled the camera out again hoping to snap it in this perfect truffle-hunting posture. So occupied had I been with the photo and with sizing up his property, I'd barely noticed when the Frenchman shuffling down the path a few steps ahead of me had plucked a screwdriver off his back stoop as we'd passed the house. The dog continued to paw about in the leaf-covered earth, and I finally snapped the picture, still not certain what my enigmatic host had in mind.

It was only when he bent down and began jabbing the long-bladed tool into the rust-colored soil under the dog's scratching paws that the realization dawned on me. *We were truffle hunting, and the dog had picked up the scent!* Mesmerized, I bent closer too, my eyes riveted on the pebbly soil. When the President's thin fingers tightened on an unmistakable black fungus and he dropped it in my palm, the *frisson* tingled all the way down to my shoes. The Frenchman still said nothing, though I caught the flicker of a smile vanishing from his lips when my eyes finally lifted from the ebony nugget in my hand. Turning back to the dog, he dropped a small biscuit in her mouth and brushed the dirt off his pants, then followed as she moved deeper into the woods.

When we returned to his house a half-hour later, I held two more of the prized fungi. It was the end of the season, the Président muttered crustily, punctuating the implicit apology with that what-can-you-say, *c'est la vie* shrug. The Lalbenque market would continue for another three or four weeks, at best. I stared down again at the trio of mushrooms. The first we'd found was the largest, nearly the size of a golf ball. The thrill I'd felt at its unearthing continued to tingle in my chest.

Almost a year before, driving through the night with my friend Bruce to our favorite steelhead river in Wisconsin, we'd had that long discussion on thrill-seeking that I alluded to above. As always when we were together, the dispute was passionate but amiable, a distant echo of the dorm-room bull sessions of our youth. This one had begun with our irreconcilable political differences, drifted on to the even wider gulf in our views of religion, and finally arrived at the gates of heaven itself. What did he envision the place as being like, I asked my born-again, oldest friend, a question as sincere as I knew his response would be.

"It will be like nothing anybody since the Creation has ever experienced," he answered after a long, contemplative pause. I didn't have to press him to continue. Life would be perfect, he went on. There would be no pain or suffering. The trees would bloom with fruit, the land with flowers impossible to imagine, the rivers run forever through gin-clear pools filled with silvery fish beyond anyone's wildest dreams. And will the elect catch them, I asked, admittedly a bit less seriously. Absolutely, he shot back quickly—"you'll catch one on every cast."

If the last question had been light-hearted, my response was not. I couldn't imagine a heaven more boring, I told him honestly. And I still can't. It was where I felt most isolated from him, and from so many of my countrymen—this apparent conviction that one can never have too much. My own perspective had been shaped early on by Thoreau, and later by Leopold. At its core lay the paradoxical fact that less was often more, from a striptease to a river filled with steelhead. "Many men go fishing all their lives without knowing it's not fish they're after," Thoreau had put it with his typical acuity. The handful of black nuggets Margot had led me to would weigh immeasurably more in memory than the thousand she might have found under more prolific oak trees. Or from Emily Dickinson's starker perspective, edged with her eye for paradox, "Success is counted sweetest by those who ne'er succeed." The truth of those simple, eloquent words had long struck me as among the most profound in American literature. Yet in exploring the poem with college classes over three decades, I'd found only a handful of students whose interpretation, when I asked them to reflect on her meaning, varied much from "All the things you want mean more if you have to work for them." Occasionally the misreading sprang from their unfamiliarity with the archaic *ne'er*, but far more often it seemed simply to reflect a knee-jerk equation of *success* with acquisition and accumulation. Coming up short in a lifetime of obsessive quests to "comprehend a nectar," in the poet's brilliant phrase, was obviously painful. Far less obvious, or so it increasingly seemed listening to my classes discuss the lyric, was its implied Leopoldian corollary that the closer one came to *never* the more the nectar meant.

The subject returned to my thoughts often through the remainder of the trip. For nearly everywhere I stopped, by comparison with my native country, the operative word was *small*. The streets and hallways were narrow, the cars compact, the hotel rooms and shower stalls barely half the size of those back home in the United States. And it wasn't only in the antique villages. The Lilliputian size of Pierre Affre's office in Paris remained firmly lodged in my memory, as did a newspaper article revealing that the average apartment size in the city had shrunk from 49 to 47 meters in the last ten years.

If such economies of scale inconvenienced and sometimes visibly annoyed many of my fellow visitors from America, they touched me with the magic wand of nostalgia—reminded me of the way it had once been in our own land, in part because so many unhealthy, supersized temptations weren't beckoning every moment to try my undisciplined soul. I'd spent much of the previous year in a failed struggle to lose ten pounds, for example, yet found myself buckling my belt a notch tighter only a few days after landing in Paris. I watched far less junk television simply because the glut of options wasn't available, walked more because of the six-dollar-a-gallon price of gasoline.

It wasn't that the French were inherently more virtuous. But conditioned reflex can lead to virtue, just as a world-view that valued size and material wealth as the ultimate marks of achievement fostered insatiable acquisitiveness. And however much the Las Vegas allure of my country's celebrated excesses might sometimes glitter in the eyes of Europeans, it was clear that many of them were quietly bewildered, even appalled, by what "American values" had come to mean.

It was not an easy impression to counter. Though my post-election angst had largely evaporated, my concern over America's political leadership had only deepened with the distance I was removed from it, for from the vantage point of Europe it was achingly clear how it fed and exploited an arrogant insularity as if it were synonymous with both freedom and the American Dream.

Twenty-five years earlier, not long after I first set foot on foreign soil, I'd wheeled my longsuffering first wife and our then very young children down a remote road in northern Scotland. It was early October. A dancing river shimmered enticingly beneath us in the sun. The still not fully resolved emotional complexities of that long-ago afternoon rose to blindside me as Monsieur Vincens' truffle-laced woods faded in my rearview mirror. For then too I had been in the grip of an obsession. I had never caught an Atlantic salmon. Several days of increasingly hopeless inquiry along Scotland's famed, impossibly expensive Highland rivers had slammed the prospect shut in my face. But this was a lesser water, and I had finally located a Scot, a village hotel owner, who not only agreed to arrange a day's beat for me but lent me a rod and half a dozen beautifully tied flies into the bargain. After a couple of tense minutes of marital negotiation, my wife dropped me off at a stone bridge below the hotel, then spent the rest of the day killing time with our two sons while I fished.

The intensity of the experience made it one of the most thrilling days of my life. Yet in those self-absorbed hours, my world contracted to the mesmeric dimensions of a fish, very little separated me from the most driven corporate C.E.O. or steroid-juiced athlete. I knew further that years of similar obsessiveness had been a primary cause of the strained, distant relationship I'd long had with my older son. He had ultimately handled it well, gone on to a rewarding academic career as a research geologist, and we had eventually grown much closer. But the guilt remained, as did psychic scars I'm probably not capable of acknowledging, even now.

Grappling with it all as I drove on, I came to a roundabout marked with one of the most ubiquitous signs on French roads: "*Vous n'avez pas la priorité.*" The directive was another haunting echo out of a vanished past. Though rarely expressed in words, it had been a psychological imperative as much taken for granted in the America I grew up in as table grace or the taboo on dirty jokes in the presence of women: *You don't have the priority.* It felt light years away from the neocons' brave new nation—from a government that routinely treated the rest of the world as if we did.

That glittering day in Scotland clung to my thoughts as I drove on through the French woods. I had hooked a single fish in my eight hours on the river, a big, stubborn salmon that remained a pulsing throb at the end of my fly line for a full hour before finally breaking off. I knew the time because I'd glanced at my watch soon after I hooked it, as I did once more in the heartsick moment the rod went dead in my hand. In the nearly three decades that had evaporated between that electric experience and the previous autumn, I'd had the chance to wade a salmon river on several other occasions. But I had never caught one, had in fact had only a single other strike.

Then, in September of 2004 on Quebec's Gaspé peninsula, I finally caught one of the elusive fish that had so long obsessed me, silver as the glint of a moonbeam and fresh out of the sea. It wasn't large, barely five pounds, no more than a third the size of the fish I'd lost all those years earlier in Scotland. And it was the only strike I had in three days of casting a fly from dawn to dark. But the frisson still comes whenever I think of it. And if some paradise ever offers the choice between such a long-dreamed-of experience and ten thousand successive strikes, I hope I'll retain enough Leopold wisdom to choose the first.

In retrospect, the gut-level drives that pushed me to Lalbenque, like those that led to that first Atlantic salmon, have brought immeasurable pleasure to my life, and considerable pain. I see my older son now, caught up in his own passionate obsessions, and feel both a paternal pride at the spirit and grit that fuel his arduous research in the hinterlands of western China and misgivings over a lifestyle I modeled for him from the day he was born. The pride is both personal and patriotic, grounded in deep appreciation of a culture whose historical veneration of self-fulfillment is surely one of the many sentiments behind *"Proud to be an American,"* the bumper sticker almost as ubiquitous on U. S. highways as the stern reminder at roundabouts throughout France. But the latter caution lingers—"*vous n'avez pas la priorité.*" In my own image of heaven, it greets all of us at the gate.

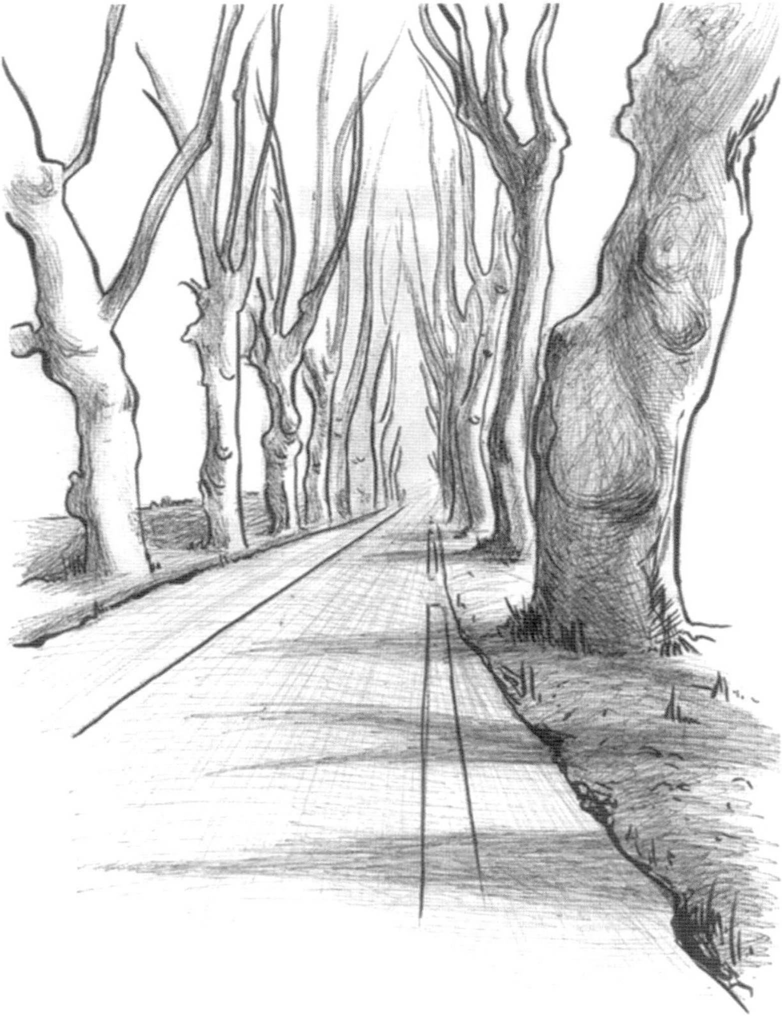

Chapter 7
Oc

Paris had been drizzly, Arromanches assaulted by a biting Channel wind, the snow-dusted streets of Souillac and Cahors chilled by temperatures that rarely rose more than a degree or two above freezing. I'd been favored with an unexpectedly rich variety of experiences in all of them, but the ceaseless cold had finally worn me down. Hoping to find less frigid weather, I left the French uplands and impulsively headed for a place I hadn't included on the trip itinerary, a small city that beckoned irresistibly on the Mediterranean shore.

Fringed by the sea and reedy marshlands that fed the latticework of inlets and marinas at its heart, Sète wore its ancient heritage as a fishing port with a louche, raffish allure. Dozens of weathered boats lined the harbor, and hundreds of smaller craft bobbed in the greenish waters as I ambled the sloping streets. Having lived for years on the upper Mississippi, I'd long been captivated by waterfront towns, and Sète remained as seductive as I remembered it. I would have holed up there for its salty air and fresh *fruit de mer* alone, but the inertia that held me for days was as much mental as physical. A little more than an hour north lay the tiny village I'd once known far better than any other in France, and I wasn't yet prepared to return.

More than a decade had passed since Jane and I spent nearly two months of a sabbatical leave in a cramped, drab gray apartment just off its featureless main square. Though it was spring, the weather then too had been unseasonably cold. Unlike several neighboring villages, Montpeyroux had no restaurant or inn, not even a cozy café or bistro. The situation was made worse, for both of us, by the fact that I had arranged the experience—a decision blindly arrived at a continent away, months previous—and by a fluky coincidence that had made the village our next sabbatical stop after three sun-splashed weeks in an Italian villa named *Bramasole*, the house lovingly described by its owner, Frances Mayes, in her celebrated memoir *Under The Tuscan Sun*. The author and her husband, an accomplished poet born and raised in the Minnesota town Jane and I lived in, had graciously rented the villa to us shortly before the book was published. Taking shameless advantage, we'd idled through those idyllic days glorying in the villa's frescoed rooms and verandas, wandering through the scenic campagne, and lingering at night in the nearby village of Cortona for its lively street life and terrific food. Looking back at the experience from the chill, almost windowless Montpeyroux apartment, the perspective was basically that of Adam and Eve gazing at Eden from outside the walls.

Once, when we'd been settled in the place long enough for the grim reality of our two-month lease to have registered, I stared out at the endless rain soaking the street and made a half-hearted stab at perspective, or what my unhappy wife would have called spin. "Contrast value," I said. "Aldo Leopold.... If you don't know pain, there's no such thing as pleasure." Whatever she muttered in response was muffled by the drumming of the rain on the slate rooftop. Even I had to admit, if only to myself, that the principle worked better when the pleasure *followed* the pain.

It took awhile, but the village's quiet rhythms and our daily walks through the vine-covered countryside helped us gradually put the letdown behind us, and we began to see what Montpeyroux offered, rather than what it did not. Jane never quite got there, but by the end of our stay I'd grown fond of the dour little hamlet and its inhabitants, rooted like the nearby upland's gnarled oaks under the relentless mistral wind.

My greater appreciation of the place wasn't a matter of toughness. A native of Manhattan, Jane could remain unruffled in a city's steamy gridlock when I was literally gasping for air and desperate to flee. The difference in Montpeyroux was that I recognized it—had once *lived* it—as she had lived her childhood a few blocks from Times Square. The pair of rustic little towns I'd grown up in were surrounded by corn and wheat fields, not vineyards. Grain elevators rather than large co-op tanks filled with local wine rose above their dusty streets. Yet the stores on Montpeyroux's square, what few stores there were, felt much the same as Guide Rock's and Silver Creek's once had when you entered, and the wine growers labored on year after year in their tiny vineyards as the farmers of my youth had tended their small farms. Nobody I knew ever got rich in the hamlets of rural Nebraska, and I doubted if anyone had in this remote French village. Not at least in recent memory. Montpeyroux's past was a different story. It stretched back to Celto-Roman times, and the crumbling ruins of a feudal chateau on a nearby hilltop, from which the village took its name, still drew the occasional historian or archaeologist to the region. But for me it had the unmistakable feel of a place inhabited by gritty, hard-working people like those I'd known on the American plains. I was painfully familiar with what time had done to those villages. The images stuck in my mind's eye every time I thought of my imminent return to Montpeyroux,

And so I lingered on in Sète, a procrastination made all too easy by its abundant, slightly seedy charms. Yet the little Languedoc village where I had once spent most of an inclement spring kept gnawing at me. Not the way Souillac and Cahors had in the days before I'd revisited them. They had appeared to be doing okay on my previous visits and I had little doubt, which proved to be justified, that they would still. Montpeyroux was different. Jane and I had inhabited it long enough to learn that even back then its *artisan boulangerie* was threatened by the corporate *Intermarché* in the larger, neighboring town of Gignac, whose croissants were markedly inferior but half a franc cheaper. And the down-at-the-heels little general store on the square was clearly imperiled as well.

I had returned to France with the belief, or at least the fervent hope, that its campagne had preserved a vibrancy now only a faded memory in most of rural America. And despite the encouraging signs from the Dordogne and Quercy, I couldn't shake my forebodings about Montpeyroux. The crisis in the French wine industry that the Dols had described to me was not yet front-page international news, as it was destined to become a few months later. There had as yet been no blockades of government agricultural offices by angry winegrowers and farmers, none of the demonstrations that would fill the streets of Béziers and Narbonne with more than 10,000 protesters while thousands more marched in Nîmes under a banner reading "*Faren tot peta, gardaren li vigno*"—Occitan for "We will blow everything up but keep the vineyards." All of that was still to come. But *Mondovino* and other facts I'd picked up since meeting the Dols increasingly worried me. Few places in the world relied more on wine for their livelihood than the cluster of Languedoc villages in the Hérault valley just north of Béziers. Vineyards, many of them scarcely larger than a *boules* court, met your eyes wherever you turned.

That elemental importance of wine to the local economy lay at the heart of my fondest Montpeyroux memory—the trek I'd made from our squat little dwelling to the communal *Cave des Vignerons* a couple of times each week. Barely two blocks away, the co-op was the single brightly painted site in the village. I was never sure from how far away other people had come as we all waited patiently in the salesroom to refill our motley array of containers. All I knew was that the wine was good, it was dirt-cheap, and you could bring anything from an empty thermos to a ten-gallon barrel and the nonchalant woman at the pump, after asking what variety you wanted, would insert her nozzle and give you a fill with the same casual insouciance Hilbert Roback had pumped ethyl into the family Packard back in Silver Creek fifty years before. Once, plastic bottle in hand, I'd watched her fill four outsized crockery jugs for a spry old man who grunted his thanks, deftly corked them, and wheeled them out on a creaking dolly. Somehow I managed to survive those two months without liver failure, I'm not sure how.

How much of all that was left, I wondered nostalgically, the marshes of Sète finally fading in my rearview mirror. Clearly the crackdown on excessive alcohol consumption the Dols had mentioned was a good thing, and no doubt long overdue, but the economic threat it and other recent changes posed to the embattled winemaking villages throughout France was considerable. I vividly remembered another of them, Aniane, a focal point of the haunting film Pierre

Affre had directed me to in Paris. Jane and I had often ambled its narrow streets, relaxed in a favorite little café on the shaded square, once sat enchanted by an orchestra recital in its ancient *église*, the nave packed to overflowing with local residents. The resilient little village, less than ten miles from Montpeyroux, had come off in *Mondovino* as a kind of communal hero, holding off the predatory corporate invaders under the leadership of its communist mayor. But for how long, I wondered, and at what eventual cost to the small vintners who had refused to sell their land?

Packing for the trip back in Minnesota, the night before my flight, I'd come across an old leaflet from that two-month stay in Montpeyroux a decade earlier. I glanced at it again as I drove on. The region's chalky pebbled soil had for centuries produced a "generous" wine, the leaflet boasted, "*riche en tannin et en couleur.*" Rich in tannin. It was the earthy taste I remembered so distinctly, a taste increasingly out of synch with the homogenized, tannin-softening alternatives more and more in favor in the new global marketplace. "It takes a poet to make a great wine," Aniane's most celebrated vintner had said poignantly in *Mondovino*. Few would have claimed greatness for the hose-pumped *vins de table* I'd toted home from the co-op in those plastic bottles, but they were no less French, and far more threatened. Dropping the leaflet back on the seat, I wondered how many of the region's lesser poets had survived.

Since Montpeyroux had no hotel, I delayed my return still another day and headed for the slightly larger Aniane, where I faintly recalled a small *Logis* tucked off the road just outside the village. But did it still exist, and if so, would it be open in the winter? The first anxiety was soon dispelled—the hotel remained where I remembered it. Parking in the empty lot, I stepped out of the car into a north wind that would have sent the hardiest, Iron Range Minnesotan in search of warmth. I had grown up with the winds of the Great Plains, three or four or seven day blows that left you with a bone-deep comprehension of how homesteaders went mad or abandoned their treeless farms to the prairie dogs and coyotes. This was that kind of wind, knifing down from the Massif Central like a nail driven into the brain. Shrinking into my jacket, I hurried toward the hotel door, silently vowing when it opened to take a room no matter what its condition or cost.

It was a decision I regretted almost at once. The scarfed, sleepy-eyed *propriétaire* at the desk was hospitable—a droll Frenchman with thinning hair and a laid-back demeanor who informed me blandly it was the coldest month the region had seen since the 1960's—but though I was his only visible lodger the room's price was the highest I'd paid since my arrival in France. Hunching out into the icy wind once more, I returned with my luggage and followed him down a frigid, dimly lit corridor to the last room at the far end. Opening the door, he handed me the key and disappeared. I pulled on a heavy sweater and glanced around the room searching for a thermostat. There didn't appear to be one—only a tiny, wafer-thin heater above the baseboard, its furrowed grooves and advanced age reminiscent of a rusted-out car radiator in a salvage lot. Cranking the dial as high as it would go, I took a book out of my duffel bag and tried to settle in. An hour later, all of it spent huddled under the bedspread as a dog barked incessantly somewhere deep in the bowels of the building, I'd finally had enough. Rankled all the more by the fact it was the first time in the trip I felt I'd been taken, I stalked back down the unlit corridor and told the impassive owner my room had no heat.

He asked if I'd turned the heater up to *Max*; nodded and gave the Gallic shrug; finally shuffled wearily out from behind the desk and returned to the room with me, saying nothing when he opened the glass door that separated the hotel's cozy lobby from the gulag of rooms lining the glacial corridor. Sighing, he bent over the heater knob for ten seconds, tapped its edge a couple of times with his middle finger, and stood up again, the resigned smile of an endlessly longsuffering innkeeper etched on his face. *Oui*, he said, the room was cold. But you must give the heater time to warm up, *monsieur*. It needs only time. If it doesn't, I will send you a woman. A practiced wink, another shrug, and he turned to leave.

It was the kind of experience, I have to admit, that would have left me fuming back in America. But a traveler learns early that you simply can't make the same judgments in France. Not at least if you want to avoid a stroke. For the bliss of the campagne is also its bane: the clock ticks several beats slower, and sometimes seems not to tick at all. Two days earlier, in a *supermarché* checkout line on the outskirts of Sète, I'd waited with three or four others, standing stoically behind me, as the clerk dealt with an overweight woman trying to buy several items that included a large clay flowerpot whose bar code stubbornly refused to register on the scanning screen. The clerk slid the pot over it several times. Nothing. Turned the heavy thing over and clumsily submitted it to a microscopic inspection. Still nothing. Finally she sent the woman back to the far end of the sprawling store for another pot as we all continued to watch. When that one too refused to register, she sent her back for a third. By now at least five minutes had passed. Still no one complained or changed lines. *C'est la vie.*

I knew grafting some of that French forbearance onto my Type A American genes was the only way to improve my lot with the blasé hotel owner. Fiddling with the heat dial, he'd seemed far more feckless than fraudulent, and maybe he was right—it needed only time. Murmuring a *merci* for his trouble, I bit my tongue and walked him to the door.

Another two hours later the room's temperature might have risen three or four degrees. Shuffling stiffly down to the dining room for dinner, I remained silent as he led me to a beautifully appointed corner table where for most of the evening I was the cozy restaurant's only guest. Seating me ceremoniously, he signaled a young waiter and handed me the carte. Not once during the amiable ritual did he mention our earlier exercise in climate control, didn't ask if my room had ever warmed.

When I bid him a slightly tipsy *bonsoir* two hours later, after finishing the complimentary glass of white wine he'd sent over from his stool at the bar, I'd spent twenty-two euros—less than thirty dollars—for food and wine that with every mouthful rose higher in the pantheon of the most delectable meals I'd ever consumed. It began with a huge mixed salad—at least a dozen ingredients, from eggs and walnuts to garden-fresh vegetables—moved on to a fork-tender *entrecôte* afloat on some ineffable bed of sauces, and culminated with an apricot tarte fringed with razor-thin slices of pineapple and kiwi, the plate glazed in a strawberry-streaked spiral of *crème anglaise* that might have swirled off the palette of Matisse. It was too much, all of it, and I felt guilty for the earlier anathema I'd silently pronounced consigning the temperature-challenged owner to Siberia. My room remained glacial, but it mattered scarcely at all.

Like so much that had lured me back to the country, the experience felt at once both indelibly foreign and weirdly familiar, as if I were simultaneously a visitor from another planet and an inhabitant of the tiny patch of earth where the alien spacecraft had touched down. For however much it exposed, from an American point of view, the inscrutability of rural French culture, I also knew—knew viscerally—what it felt like to peer out from the other side and see wide-eyed incredulity at behavior that had defined you for so long it felt the way rubbing noses must once have felt to Eskimos. "Normal" is simply the world one happens to know, and it takes a long time, even if you leave it for another, to get a genuine feel for how insular it can appear to an outsider. Where I grew up on the Plains, parents roped our sleds to the back bumpers of the family car and pulled us laughing hysterically down snow-packed country roads at thirty miles an hour; we gathered at the town dump in our jalopies on steamy summer nights to shoot rats out of the windows with .22 rifles; and before we reached those years of lofty, high-school sophistication, our biggest thrill was the mandatory monthly fire drill, when we scrambled for head-of-the-line position at the bottom of the fire escape in the almost mystical hope of glimpsing a flesh-stirring flash of panties or upper thigh as the screaming girls shot down. Long after I'd left Silver Creek, such things still felt as unexceptional as the fact that during home games our football team climbed into the rickety bleachers at halftime, still clad in our cleats and shoulder pads, to play the Kreeketeer fight song in the school band.

I checked out of the *Logis* the next morning, my gratitude for the *propriétaire*'s hospitality not quite extending to a second night spent mummy-wrapped in the thin blanket I'd found rummaging through the room's musty chest of drawers. The one-night stand didn't appear to trouble him, perhaps because he'd forgotten to send me the bed-warmer he'd promised. Sketching the route on a slip of paper, he gave me directions to the nearby vineyard I'd inquired about, adding his own detailed commentary on the matchless quality of its wines. I drove back through the village and soon found it. A passing bicyclist confirmed that it was indeed the property of Monsieur Guibert, the eloquent poet of resistance in *Mondovino*. Of several small vintners from around the world featured in the documentary, he had made the deepest impression, and I wanted to buy one or two of his creations as a symbolic tribute before I left Aniane.

The *Mas de Daumas Gassac* vineyard, tucked into thickly wooded hills down a narrow, potholed road flanked by rows of *platane* trees, produced *crus* that a host of influential wine critics had celebrated as among the best in the world. Turning off the road through the gate, I paused for a nervous moment before driving on.

A single other car was parked in the small lot beside a pair of tile-roofed, immaculately groomed buildings. I entered the salesroom as the other visitors were leaving, several individual bottles of wine cased in stylish wooden boxes in their hands. The attendant, a raven-haired Frenchwoman who introduced herself as Lydia, immediately turned her attentions to me. With a warmth and informality that quickly put me at ease, she gave a brief overview of the vineyard's history and then led me up a narrow stair to the oak-beamed tasting room, where for the next ten minutes a swelling crescendo of sublime sensations washed over my tongue.

I had just settled on a pair of reds in my modest price range when footsteps echoed on the stone stair and a white-haired, nattily-dressed Frenchman stepped into the room. His craggy face was instantly recognizable from the film. It was Monsieur Guibert.

Shaking my hand and greeting me with a courtly nod, he asked where I was from and I told him. Yes, he said, he knew Minnesota. In the past he had often made trips to the United States and knew the country well. The brief exchange was in English, and I relaxed further, my French vocabulary falling several degrees short of the arcane mysteries of the *vignoble*. For the next fifteen or twenty minutes, standing with Lydia in the quiet elegance of the comfortable old room, we continued to chat.

The weather was indeed remarkably cold for Languedoc, the old vintner confirmed. The temperature had fallen as low as minus-ten Celsius that very morning. At sixteen-below it became dangerous for the vines, he added. But March was only a few days away, and regardless, there was nothing one could do.

How large was his vineyard, I asked. "Fifty hectares," he answered. "The other fifty I give to nature. You must choose, eh? You make money or you make art."

The statement, an echo of his film comment about wine and poetry, was so matter of fact it came off not as arrogance but as a simple, incontrovertible fact. I told him I knew little about the subtleties of wine but agreed completely with his vision, and that as an American I found less and less of it in my own country. He nodded, saying nothing for some time, as if weighing his response.

"My family has done work in America for four or five generations," he finally said. "Until the 1960's we were all around your country. I used to visit it twice a year. All around. Boston, Detroit, Chicago. During that period we were in contact with deep America— *l'Amérique profonde*. These people I think were very close to us, eh? But then in the sixties the passion went out of the people. Things were not the same."

He paused again to see whether I understood him, then went on. "I think there is a big difference between America fifty years ago and today, eh? Rich gangsters. That is the biggest difference. But it is much the same in France, the people around Chirac. Too rich people. Money. We have the same problem. The population is not involved."

I asked if he thought the small vineyards of France, like his own, were threatened. "There is no doubt about that," he answered instantly. "The problem for the politician today is to make big money with the bank. For example, *Crédit Agricole*."

All I knew about the ubiquitous French bank was that you saw its familiar green and white sign everywhere, and that I had often withdrawn euros from its ATM machines. "It is a gangster bank," he went on. "It owns more land in France than anybody else. Because if somebody gets in difficulty, they take the land. They use it to make big promotion of houses, for big tourists. Money money money. I think unfortunately we are…." He left the thought unfinished, but its direction, and what it boded for the things about his country I admired most, were depressingly clear.

His indictment of the corporate profiteers again recalled *Mondovino*, and I told him I'd seen the film—respected the stand he'd taken in refusing to sell or lease his vineyard. "I am just an old man who didn't surrender," he shrugged, shaking his head.

Again the matter-of-fact way he said it moved me, and I told him I'd grown up in a pair of hamlets even smaller than Aniane—hoped the villages of France could somehow hold onto what so many in America had lost, retain the vibrancy that gave his country's *campagne* such appeal. "I am not optimistic," he responded. "We used to have twenty percent farmers, occupying the territory. Everywhere in France. Even the mountains. You have the good people, with independent brain, eh? But now, one percent." He made a sharp whistling sound, *ssssssst*, like grain dust vanishing in the wind. "The rest gone. Everywhere, money money money. One-fifth of the French population was farming fifty years ago. That means we were producing good food—bread and fruit and so on. Now, *sssssssst*, thrown away. The corporations now sell anything. They are killers, nothing else."

He paused again, shaking his head. It was the most impassioned speech I had heard, from anyone, in the nearly thirty years since I first set foot in his country. "And at the end," he resumed more softly, "they kill the farmers. That is where it finishes. When a country lose its farmers, it loses its personality…. But what can we do, eh?"

The last comment came with a stoic shrug that combined disgust, resignation, and the profound sense of loss I felt about my own native land. A brief silence filled the room. "But you are doing something," I went on, "and I admire it a lot."

"It is not a matter of admiration," he replied with a dismissive wave of his hand. "It's a matter of being faithful to your ideal. Not to money. The gangsters put in the mind of the people that it is *obligation*—this desire for riches—that they cannot be happy without more money.... I think it is a disaster, eh?"

However bad it was in France, I responded, the mindset he'd described seemed to me even more dominant in America, though I knew his country only superficially, through the eyes of a traveler, at second-hand. No, he agreed, I was right. The gangster presence was everywhere in the United States.

And is the influence—this change in France you've described—coming *from* America, I asked. "Absolutely," he answered without hesitation. "Have you read the book by Galbraith?" he asked suddenly. "Just a little book. He is ninety years old. But he writes it clearly—the powers there are gangsters and liars. Criminal liars, the rich companies that control so much."

The sound of a door opening in the salesroom downstairs echoed up the stone steps, and we quickly moved to our *au revoirs*. "We may be pessimistic now," he concluded, "but I think it will be worse in a few years. Then there will be a comeback, eh? Maybe a century from now, it will return." Smiling, he turned to leave and glanced back at Lydia. "*Une bouteille de blanc pour monsieur*," he told her as he reached the stair. "*Un cadeau.*"

It was not until later, back in Aniane, that I learned how fully the old man's actions backed up his ardent words. The fifty hectares he had "given to nature" were indeed half his property. The remaining acres were divided into more than fifty tiny clearings fringed by the surrounding *garrigue* that left the vines to soak in the wild thyme, rosemary, fennel, mint, and numerous other plants which gave his wines their distinctive old world taste. His *vignoble* used no chemical fertilizer, only natural dung compost, which along with other rejections of modern techno-chemistry reduced its annual production to less than a fifth of the new industrialized vineyards. And in perhaps the most archaic nod to tradition, his grapes were picked entirely by hand, without harvesting machinery. I had glimpsed the photographs behind him as we talked in the tasting room—a dozen laughing, high-spirited youths in group pictures snapped on sunny autumn days after they'd made *la vendange*. Plucking the fruit into baskets and reveling the night away, they were part of a ritual that went back to the Middle Ages and beyond.

Later that afternoon, I drove on to Montpeyroux. A decade gradually vanished as I crept up the winding highway out of Aniane and passed the steep limestone gorge of the Hérault. I knew that fork in the road would have led me, if I'd taken it, to the pilgrimage shrine of *St. Guilhem le Désert*. A half century ago, its cloisters had been carted away to New York City, but the site remained a marvel and I would soon revisit it. It was close enough to Montpeyroux Jane and I had once walked there down the vine-bordered route I remained on as I crossed the Hérault bridge. A few yards downstream was another bridge, more than a thousand years older, *Le Pont du Diable*, built from local stone during the same period as the pilgrimage church. I pulled off and walked back up the road to gaze down at it, reflecting on the swiftness of time's arrow, before driving slowly on.

As if on cue, my first glimpse of the familiar little village in the distance was followed almost at once by another image even more timeless than the medieval *pont*—a laborer turning up his vineyard's arid soil with a long-bladed hoe. You saw it everywhere in the south of France, or had the last time I'd been there, before *la crise* and wine's new industrialized frontier. Slowing instinctively, I pulled off as far as I could on the foot-wide shoulder and climbed out of the car once more.

The man stared at me and leaned patiently on his hoe as I approached through the closely cropped rows of gnarled vines, either bemused by my abrupt road-clogging stop or grateful for the break from his backbreaking labor. Unfortunately, in my impulsive urge to speak with him I had momentarily forgotten that the derivation of *Languedoc* was "the language of *Oc*," the fiercely proud and independent region's time-honored name. Our first night in the village, that swift decade earlier, Jane and I had spent an hour struggling to penetrate the ancient French dialect in a futile attempt to learn from our rented apartment's aged caretaker how to run the wash machine and switch on the gas stove. Though my French had improved since then, I grasped almost nothing of what the old man in the vineyard said to me, though he remained friendly, even voluble, throughout our exchange. As brown and gnarled as his vines, he punctuated his responses to my questions with a full register of grunts and nods accented with periodic thrusts of a calloused thumb. I caught only that he owned ten hectares of land, all of it in the vineyard we stood in except the squat house he pointed to in the distance, and that being a *vigneron* meant "*beaucoup de travail.*" Did it earn him a decent living, I asked, as I had asked the Dols several days earlier. "*Vous gagnez la vie?*" He smiled wanly and glanced down at the upturned earth, still leaning on the sweat-darkened hoe. "*Difficile,*" he grunted. "*Très difficile.*"

I thanked him for his time and crept the last kilometer on into the village, past several other vineyards even smaller, relieved that this distinctive feature of the place, at least, remained. Postage-stamp plots of vines still encircled the town, a few of the tiniest actually *in* the town, squeezed into the narrow spaces between buildings. At first glance the buildings too looked much as I remembered them. The little *artisan boulangerie* remained on the square, though a *fermée* sign hung in the window when I parked and approached it. The pock-marked, ramshackle old *Alimentation Générale* on the corner showed a few more age-lines than I remembered, but it appeared to have held on as well. A hand-lettered sign taped inside the door said it would be open from *16:30 a 19:00*, and I made a mental note to return then.

In the meantime, I wandered the sunless streets that spoked off the central square, gray corridors of stone and stucco so cramped I'd once nearly gotten our car wedged in one of them, before swallowing my pride and backing the fifty yards out past an elderly woman who stared sympathetically at Jane through her kitchen window, mere inches away. Though I'd struck no woodpile or fire hydrant on that occasion, the memory was as wistful as that of the Rabbitman.

I walked on toward the village outskirts, down the street I'd always taken on my daily morning runs, hoping without expecting to come to the old house with a chicken-wire fence where the militant tom turkey had gobbled threateningly at me whenever I'd passed. The house remained, but both the coop and the bird were gone, as was the *"Occitanie Libre!"* scrawled in faded red paint on a rock face just beyond the town.

I walked back with an almost prayerful gratitude that so much else in the village felt the same. Even the piercing, late afternoon chill rekindled memories of Jane huddling grimly by the puny fire in our rented apartment. I'd passed the building an hour earlier— paused and briefly considered knocking on its familiar, blue-painted door. But the impulse died almost as soon as it was born. Whoever the thick limestone walls now sheltered would remain as unknown to me as the impenetrable speech of the old *vigneron* with the hoe.

Returning to the square, I drifted on to the wine co-op, its quintet of silo-sized holding tanks brightly splashed with painted grapes and vines. Two or three locals lounged just inside the door, eyeing me with that tight-lipped curiosity any approaching stranger evoked from the resident geezers who hung out on the tavern "Liars Benches" of my youth. My home town had been almost invisibly small, the archetypal stoplight-less "blink and you miss it" boondock, but in that pre-Interstate era of American history it pulsed with a road and rail life the little wine co-op brought back with an almost painful recall. Both the Union Pacific and one of the nation's major east-west arterials, the "Lincoln Highway," had bisected Silver Creek, giving us a sense of place and significance in a fixed universe that brought tears of incredulous laughter to a sardonic new friend's eyes, a few years later, when I mentioned the fact to him my first semester in graduate school. He was a temporary academic transplant from Queens, and I'd made the naïve mistake of asking him what people in New York thought of Nebraska. His answer was as immediate as it was brutally honest: "They don't."

Eventually I also came to see my native village with some of that cool, objective distance, though I remained unsure the change was entirely a good thing. And the perspective took a long time to come. Nodding to the duffers in the wine co-op as I walked past them, I recalled an incident from my final year of crop adjusting—a scorching summer afternoon when I sat in my car killing an hour on a dusty village street before my next appointment at an outlying farm. Not a soul was visible. Nothing moved in the midday heat but a few sparrows pecking at seeds on the cracked sidewalk. Aside from a few scattered houses, the entire town seemed to consist of the post office, a grain elevator, and a run-down bar. How could anybody live in such a godforsaken place, I wondered. It never occurred to me that Silver Creek, less than thirty miles distant, held barely two hundred more souls.

"Thirty," as we called the busy highway that flowed through our tiny village, had made all the difference, a route that held magic for me even before I read *On The Road* and learned it was Kerouac's path through the nation's heart. The highway gave Silver Creek both its character and its sense of identity, and when Interstate-80 was built in the 60's—the decade Monsieur Guibert had singled out as the time everything changed in America—the village's sharp decline followed almost at once. The shriveled flow of traffic, and the lost business it had generated, fused with the depopulation effected by increased farm size and mechanization to make our main street a shell of what it formerly had been. My hometown soon lost both its motels, a pair of cafés, two butcher shops and a drugstore where kids had drifted away from the free shows in the park to congregate for malts and flirtatious dalliance every Saturday night. A lone, depleted grocery survived where two had fed and mostly clothed the village during my childhood. The closed store, Bordys', had been owned by an elderly Jewish couple as sociable as they were alien on the prairie. The village back then was so rigidly Christian and sectarian the single-block distance between the Catholic and Methodist churches held the psychological weight of the Berlin Wall. Most people in town supported both grocery stores more or less equally nonetheless, and the Bordys had made a go of it until Sam died and his wife moved back East to be closer to their son.

I had returned to Silver Creek often in the decades since on short visits to my mother, and knew that its close-knit sense of community hadn't died. There were simply far fewer opportunities to express it. What remained of the once lively downtown was little more than the scaled-down grocery and a pair of ratty, evolution-proof bars.

Pausing by the unoccupied sales-desk of the wine co-op, I recalled the many times I'd stood there, ten years before. The attractive little building remained Montpeyroux's lifeblood as surely as the transcontinental highway from New York to San Francisco had been my native village's, the tiny vineyards that fed it as essential as cornfields were to rural Nebraska's communal pulse. Having feared the worst, I was delighted to see that here too not much since my sabbatical stay in the town seemed to have changed.

The co-op attendant, a stern, sharp-featured man in his forties, stood attentively at one of the four hoses filling a container for the room's only other apparent client, and I remained by the desk waiting patiently for the transaction to end. After the purchases and gifts of the previous few days the last thing I needed was more wine, but for nostalgia's sake I had rummaged under the car seat and brought in an empty liter water bottle. It felt good simply to hang back and watch the familiar proceedings. So much in the room remained unchanged, in fact, I was totally unprepared for the rude awakening I was about to receive. When my turn came and I approached the mustached attendant, he shook his head before I could say a word, wagging his finger in that inimitable French way that looks to American eyes like the scolding of a prudish schoolmistress. "No containers like zat," he said sternly in English, turning to another customer who had just entered the room. I slouched confusedly away trying not to look at the clutch of grinning locals, the taboo vessel dangling from my hand.

Licking my wounds, I retreated to the far side of the room, searching for a sign that might explain whatever code I had violated. Bottles and cases of wine were neatly stacked at half a dozen locations on the gleaming floor tiles. Tasting glasses sparkled on a circular counter. On the far wall, a list of the coop's *crus* hung impressively, a brief description of their respective qualities and prices attached. What the hell, I thought, abandoning the search for enlightenment. The guy speaks English. And who else was I likely to find who would know as much as he would about the current state of things in the town?

Eventually the room cleared again of other buyers and I approached him once more, this time determined to buy one of the reds the wall chart had listed—at slightly over ten euros a bottle the priciest the co-op sold. A decade earlier, the pumped varieties had cost barely a dollar a liter, and I'd glimpsed enough in my brief fiasco with the water bottle to know that even now they were less than five. Whether from improved taste or lingering embarrassment, I cleared my throat and told him I'd like to try the *Château de Roquefeuil.*

He nodded stiffly and walked over to a pair of opened bottles on a table behind the desk. Pouring some of each, he studied me intently as I just as intently sniffed, swirled, and did my best impression of a connoisseur letting the wines work on my tongue. I told him I preferred the first, the wine I'd selected. It was in fact genuinely so good I impulsively added that I'd changed my mind—would take two bottles. Grunting approval, he took a pair from off a shelf and packaged them, his severe expression easing noticeably. No one else had entered the store or required his immediate attentions, and he appeared open to conversation. It wasn't long before I raised the issue that had occupied my thoughts for several days.

Several people had told me there was a wine crisis in France, I said, but I remained uncertain of the reasons. "There are two reasons," he responded at once. His tone remained professorial, the lofty voice of a lecture hall, and I gradually realized his demeanor was far less impolite than simply the mark of painstaking care. "Ze first is the law," he continued. "One can drink only a *maximum* of two small glasses if you will be driving. As a result ze people drink much less now. Ze gendarmes stop them at ze edge of every town and village. And when you cannot drive your car, you are a finished man." The pause which followed as he peered at me to let that unassailable truth sink in over the top of his glasses had the weight of an inscribed stone. "Ze second reason is the wine outside of France, on ze world market," he went on. "Chile. *Australie.* South Africa. A new product with fantastic bottles, pretty labels, and yes, I must admit, not so very bad of quality. Ze difference is in France we use a blend of different grapes. It is not easy to make French wine. Ze procedure is more *compliquée,* more expensive. Ze cheaper foreign wines are more one wine, one grape."

Earlier, glancing over the various blends on the wall chart when he'd been occupied with other customers, I'd noticed that Syrah composed less than three percent of the *Cuvée d'Or* the co-op proudly dubbed its "Classic Montpeyroux Red." Scarcely five years earlier, Syrah was a virtual non-presence in the Minnesota and Wisconsin wine marts I frequented. Now Australian imports with cuddly animal labels filled the shelves. Though I didn't much like them, I'd bit back the urge to comment when they appeared, as they had more and more often, as the wine of choice at the dinner parties of friends.

My next question as a result came with considerable foreboding. Had the exploding global popularity of the varietals seriously threatened the Montpeyroux market, I asked.

Not seriously—yet—he answered. The co-op's reputation was excellent and it sold all over the world, especially in Canada. And it had begun selling its own varietals with fair success. "Ze same as the Chilean wines," he smiled shrewdly, a bottle from under the counter materializing in his hand. "We are having no big problem here, but in France in general it is very hard."

I asked him finally how many local winegrowers the co-op sold for, something I'd never thought to wonder about in my frequent visits to the *cave* a decade before. There were 170 *vignerons*, he answered, owning a total of 600 hectares, plus thirteen *domains* adding some 200 hectares more. The former figure startled me. I'd long known the sea of vineyards surrounding the little village had numerous individual owners—that the ancient French laws against primogeniture had led to ever-smaller estates—but an average of eight acres per holding seemed a striking French equivalent of what even back in my Nebraska youth had been called a "small farm," usually the traditional quarter section, or "quarter" of land. And if one discounted the dozen or so Montpeyroux vintners who each owned fifteen or twenty hectares, it left an average of no more than five or six acres for all the rest. The collection of hard facts, taken together, painted an economic future as grim as I'd been told.

It was impossible not to think again of *Mondovino*, and I asked the wineseller if he thought the neighboring village's resistance to the corporate invaders would have any longterm effect. "It is too late, I think," he responded, shaking his head resignedly. "I hope I am someday wrong."

I walked back to the square and dropped the wine in my car, then walked on to the little store on the corner, a light now shining through the dusty windowpane. Too many years before to count, back in Guide Rock, Nebraska, my grandmother had often sent me downtown to a similar establishment when she needed a spool of thread or some additional salt to freeze the ice cream we hand-cranked until our muscles burned. To a child's eyes the old general store, Fringer's, held a small universe under the slow-turning wood-bladed fan that hung from its dented tin ceiling: tilted barrels filled with screws and nails, union suits with button bottoms, a Flexible Flyer dangling on a hook above the door. The proprietor was a curt, no-nonsense little man whose squirrel-bright eyes glinted behind wire-rimmed glasses. Once, when I was nine or ten and already mad about fishing, I read an article in *Field & Stream* on the latest whiz-bang improvement of the fishing hook. A bristly set of barbs and a humped shank gave the hook an exaggerated profile that resembled a kind of squat, snub-nosed porcupine. After I'd harassed my father mercilessly to buy a box of them, he finally flipped me a quarter and shooed me away. "Go down and see if old man Fringer has any of 'em," he muttered, suppressing a grin.

He knew the storekeeper's legendary grouchiness put an intimidating quiver in my loins, but the weirdly curved hooks gleamed like fool's gold in my mind's eye, and I dutifully rode my bike down to the store. A lump in my throat, I tried vainly for several minutes to describe them to him, his bony frame bent stiffly toward me over an ancient glass case filled with catfish tackle and sealed jars of stink-bait. The tongue-tied words did nothing but pull the drawstring furrows even tighter around his lips.

"All my hooks are bent," he finally stopped me. "I don't carry no straight ones. And none of them porky-pines neither, son."

In memory, neither had the little Montpeyroux store when Jane and I had last filled a shopping bag in its cramped interior, but shoes and socks and sealing wax were a good bet, along with dozens of other items on its worn counters and shelves. Stepping through the door, I saw at once that the store was diminished, though hanging on doggedly. There were still scattered boxes of fruits and vegetables, assorted canned goods stacked on the now emptier shelves, even a row of open baskets and burlap sacks filled with produce on the chipped, peeling floor. Along the cluttered aisle, an illuminated glass case not unlike old man Fringer's shone with assorted cheeses, sausages, and a number of other charcuterie items. It alone remained exactly as I remembered it, down to the hand-written prices on slips of white paper stabbed into the meat. A middle-aged clerk emerged from a back room to serve me warbling a cheery *bonjour*, wiping her plump hands on a blue apron as she approached. When places like this are gone, I thought, part of France's soul will have died as well.

I bought a thick slice of the *pâté de campagne* and waited as the woman wrapped it in butcher paper, then drove out of town on a street I knew would take me past the only remembered site I hadn't yet revisited, a memorial to those who'd died in the last century's two world wars. You saw the weathered monuments in village squares everywhere throughout the country, often fringed with fresh or faded flowers, "*Mort Pour La France*" or similar words inscribed on the base. The Montpeyroux obelisk also read "*À Nos Héros*" at its crown, above the lists of dead chiseled into the stone. Parking, I got out and walked slowly around the monument's four tapered sides, reading the names. There were fifty-three of them, from a village of slightly more than eight hundred people. I stood for a time in silence, near a withered bouquet someone had left, recalling the joke I'd heard back home about French cowardice—the vintage rifle that had been dropped once, but never fired.

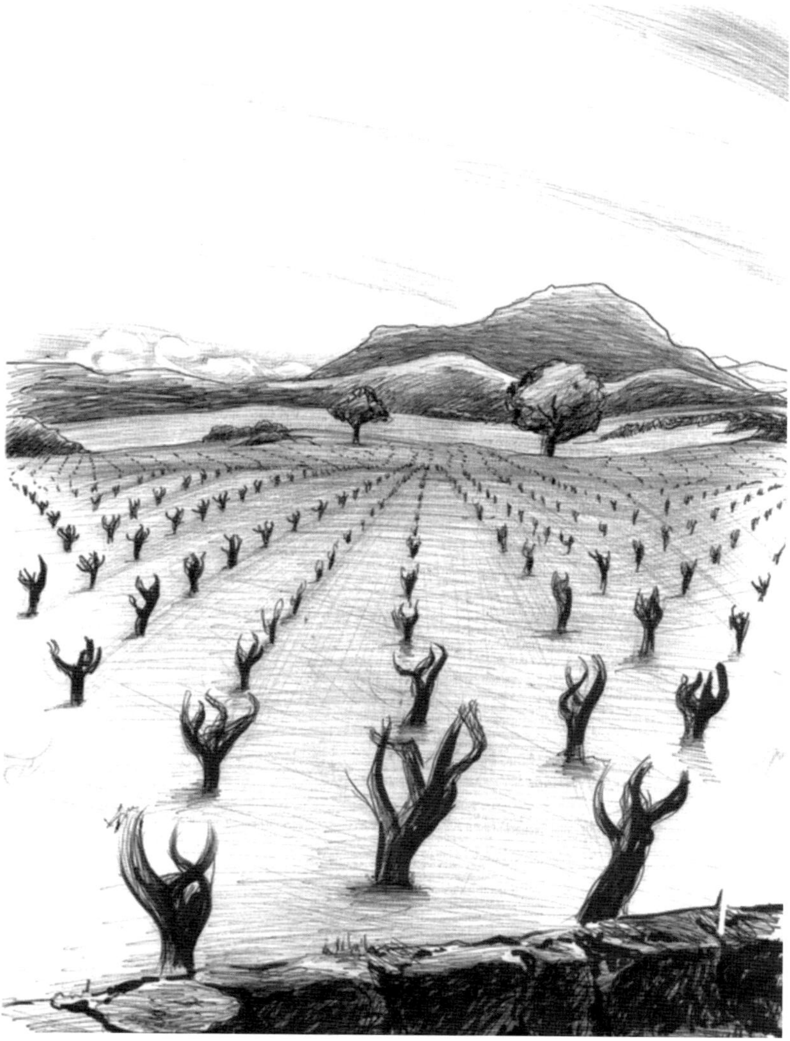

Chapter 8
Kissing The Gods

I drove on through the vineyards in the gathering dusk following the crooked road to the village of Saint Saturnin, its squat, earth-colored dwellings tucked at the foot of the sheep-pastured uplands that rose over the broad valley of the Hérault. The village was even tinier than Montpeyroux, but I remembered it fondly for the quiet beauty of its square and a fine, smoke-darkened restaurant beneath the largest of its ancient plane trees. The two villages were less than five miles apart, but each had its own communal *cave* that fed a rivalry as full-blooded as it was entrenched in the region's long history. An Englishman who lived in the smaller village had once described it to me. Not long after he moved there, he said, he'd casually mentioned to a neighbor that earlier in the afternoon he'd been down to Montpeyroux to sample its vintages. The grizzled resident grunted contemptuously and spat in the dust. "If you drink another drop," he said, "I do not speak to you again."

The village remained as quiet as I remembered it, though the closely cropped *platane* trees were leafless and the *place* empty of other cars. The restaurant appeared to be open, a huge relief since I knew of no other anywhere near. Anticipating the meal throughout the day, I'd eaten nothing but a few pieces of fruit for breakfast, and the chalked *carte* on the slate by the door was exactly what I'd hoped to see. Half a dozen fetching *plats principals* were scrawled semi-legibly, and I was ravenous enough to order them all.

A tall, loose-jointed man with a scruffy salt and pepper beard sat hunched over a cluttered desk as I entered, a cell phone in his hand. Briefly glancing up at me, he turned back to the conversation I'd interrupted. The owner I remembered had been older, the restaurant's smoky interior painted a garish purple, but the place otherwise looked much the same as it had a decade before. A log lay ready for burning in the blackened fireplace. The same wine-stained wooden stools ringed the small entryway bar.

I stood patiently by the door as the apparent new owner remained on the phone. Five minutes later, he finally signed off and turned back to me. "*Oui, monsieur?*" he said languidly, his shaggy eyebrows lifting above his thin, stubbled face. I asked if I could have a table for dinner, feeling slightly absurd given the emptiness of the place. "I am sorry," he answered in French, "but in the winter we are not open on weekday evenings. Only at lunchtime. Perhaps you can come back Friday or Saturday night."

That was unfortunately not possible, I said. I was simply passing through, had stopped because his restaurant was one I'd particularly enjoyed when my wife and I had lived briefly in Montpeyroux, ten years earlier. His keen, heavy-lidded eyes registered a mild interest, and he switched abruptly to English. Despite his louche, irrepressibly continental demeanor, he was so fluent and colloquial the language might have been his native tongue.

"Yes," he nodded, clearly pleased when I told him so. "I learned English long ago. I am German, though I've lived here for some time. My wife and I bought the restaurant eight years ago. Before that I was a builder. I sold properties. You learn whatever you need to survive."

"So tell me," he abruptly changed the subject, "what part of America are you from?"

I hadn't told him I was an American, but had long ago ceased being surprised by the recognition. Spend months abroad and you still wear the fact like a chevron on your sleeve. Slouching past me to the bar, he picked up a pack of cigarettes and held it out to me. When I told him I didn't smoke, he lit up and took a long, lip-tightening drag, the question still hanging in the air.

The guy had an aging hippie look that suggested years of inhalations considerably more exotic than tobacco, and I geared myself down to the same laid-back key.

"I'm from the Midwest," I said nonchalantly. "Minnesota. A little town about a hund—"

His response was electric—close to unhinged. In the argot of the era he gave every sign of still inhabiting, the dude went absolutely ape-shit. "*Minnesota!*" he cut me off. "*Bob Dylan! Dylan is God!*"

The next few minutes passed in a blue haze of cigarette smoke so viscous the long-haired bohemian might have been a presence I'd conjured out of the air. His name was Pius, he told me, bestowed on him by his devout mother at his birth in 1958, the year of the Pope's death. "I give you my blessing," he added drolly, raising a limp hand over my head as he slouched past me again and plucked a bottle of white wine from behind the bar. Uncorking it, he poured each of us a brimming glass and rolled on.

No, there was no genius like Dylan, he repeated, with the possible exception of Jimmie Hendrix. Jimmie was Mozart, he said reverently. Jimmie kissed the gods.

I asked him who else he liked. Lou Reed, he said. Leonard Cohen. Tom Lehrer. All of them were geniuses—true *artists*. Not quite the immortal Bob, but clearly in the first rank of the elect.

The mention of Lehrer surprised me. A Harvard mathematician turned musical satirist, his "Vatican Rag" and other wickedly clever lampoons had been staples of my graduate-school days, but were now barely known outside a mostly academic coterie of fervent admirers, even in the U.S. Yet the gangly pope of Saint Saturnin seemed to be filled with such obscure bits of knowledge, and refilling our glasses with the crisp local wine, he continued to pontificate on topics that ranged from the mysteries of Zen to the art of making a good brick.

Curious about his take on the issues that had absorbed me in Montpeyroux and Aniane, I took advantage of a brief pause in the conversation as he re-corked the bottle. What did he think of the region's economic future, I asked—the survival prospects of its family-owned vineyards and small businesses, like his own. They weren't bright, he responded soberly. He and his wife had lost money every year they'd owned the restaurant. And the altered drinking tastes, the foreign competition, had left the local winegrowers facing years of financial uncertainty, or worse. Saint Saturnin's co-op remained sound for the time being, he said, echoing what I'd been told in Montpeyroux two hours earlier. It had a solid market, especially in Belgium, and a longstanding reputation for good wine. But measures clearly needed to be taken. Recently there had even been some talk of merging the two villages' separate *caves* to save administrative costs and other expenses, but the idea had inevitably come to nothing. In five hundred years the rival camps had never agreed on anything.

He blew a puff of blue smoke out the side of his mouth and shook his head disgustedly, a long-suffering pontiff wearied by the absurd antics of the Calvinists and the Lutherans. The sad thing, he went on, was that the region had become wildly popular with outsiders. Real estate prices were five times what they had been a decade earlier. Two thousand people a month moved down from Paris and Lyon and other cities in the north to the Hérault. "*Two thousand a month!*" he repeated. The valley was now the most popular place to move in France. Yet villages like Saint Saturnin and Montpeyroux saw almost none of the benefits. Their economies continued to decline.

I asked him what he would do if his restaurant failed. "Become a builder again," he shrugged. "Or sell real estate. I know how to do both." I peered at him through the haze, saying nothing, his shrewd, riverboat gambler's eyes peering keenly back at me. The transplanted German's quick-wittedness left little doubt he'd land on his feet, regardless. I was far less certain that natives of the region would manage nearly as well.

Setting the emptied wine bottle aside, he opened a second and our conversation flowed on, the day's light slowly fading in the cozy little room. We talked about other musicians we both admired, books we had read, favorite writers and painters and entertainers. And then he said something that stunned me—drove home how little I truly knew of the village I'd spent almost two months inhabiting a decade before. "Ten years ago?" he mused, scratching his scraggly chin when I made a passing reference to the poet whose place Jane and I had rented. Yes, he said, he knew her. She still came to the restaurant occasionally. Her house was just up the street from the square, not far from Margot St. James's. Back then she'd had a place in Montpeyroux as well.

Margot St. James. It took a few seconds for the name to register—the flamboyant champion of prostitutes back in the heady days of feminist marches who'd founded an organization called COYOTE, an acronym for "Call Off Your Old Tired Ethics." The news felt a little like it must have felt if you lived in Hibbing, Minnesota, back in the 60's, and belatedly learned that some hotshot new folk singer was the whiny-voiced neighbor kid who used to drive you crazy bleating on his harmonica and strumming his guitar. Seeing the dazed look on my face, Pius laughed and rolled on. The writer Ian McEwen also had a house nearby, he said offhandedly—"I did some building work for him"—"and the dude that wrote *The Loneliness of the Long-Distance Runner*…uh…" He paused, groping for the name. "Alan Sillitoe," I mumbled numbly. "Yeah," he said. "He's probably dead by now but he had a place near here too. So did a bunch of other artists—Patrick Shelley the painter, the great, great grandson of the poet. A few photographers whose work you'd prob'ly know."

The front door abruptly bumped open at that point and a little girl scampered happily into the bar. "*Papa, papa!*" she squealed as he lifted her, sharing her delight at a beeping and blinking toy robot she'd dropped on the floor. Her name was Gloria, she told me proudly in French at her father's urging, and she was five years old. She asked me what my name was and I told her. Soon her mother and four-year-old sister Constanza joined us, and the snug little room took on a rollicking family air. Sounding a bit dazed himself, as if one of Jesus's disciples had dropped in on their village, Pius announced to all of them where the surprise American visitor was from. "*It's the state where Bob Dylan grew up!*" he added to his wife in French. She rolled her eyes and turned to me with a polite, resigned smile as he lifted the bottle and poured her a glass of the wine. Though she spoke almost no English, it took only a few more seconds to learn that her obvious fondness for her husband didn't extend to his musical tastes. Her own favorite was "Jeem Morrison," she informed me with emphasis, glancing cheekily back at him. "*Ze Doors—merveilleux!*" It was now the pope's turn to roll his eyes, punctuating the expression with a contemptuous grunt in a droll marital debate that had clearly played out countless times in years past. The two little girls had slipped away and gone back to the robot, which added its beeps and whistles to the clamor as it clicked stiff-leggedly across the floor.

Goose-stepping beside it, Gloria began to count their matched steps in French, then looked up at me and cried out for me to join her. Darting behind the bar, she leapt into her father's arms again, still counting. She made it into the eighties before hitting the wall, at which point Constanza insisted on showing me how far she could count too. The younger girl reached *trente-sept, quarante-neuf* before Pius kissed her to a stop and the room filled with laughter. But Gloria wasn't finished. I had to count too, she repeated. When I dutifully performed my best *un* to *dix*, she shook her head sternly, correcting my pronunciation of "*quatre*" and "*huit*."

Pius's wife, whose name I never learned in the delightful hubbub, had drifted away to begin preparing their dinner, and I rose to leave. I had already been in the restaurant far beyond the limits of hospitality, but Pius insisted that I remain and finish my wine. When his daughters disappeared too, not long after Gloria grabbed my hand and told me the robot's name was "Kent," the room fell silent. Curious what a man of such wide-ranging intellect and interests would say in answer, I asked him one last question.

With all that's recently happened in the world, I said, what are your feelings about America?

An hour earlier, when he told me he'd never been to the U.S., the fact surprised me. But I still wasn't prepared for his response. "Bush has done one good thing for Europeans," he said after a moment of reflection. "You never doubt where he stands on anything, and he's made us look at things more in that way too."

I was less sure, as his sardonic smile faded, that a statement I'd first taken as mordant irony was entirely so.

"But don't you find the way he looks at them dangerous?" I countered. "Filled with half-truths and the belief that God has chosen him to—"

He laid a bony hand on my shoulder and stopped me, the crooked grin flickering once more before vanishing from his enigmatic face. "I have my own America," he said softly. "*Bob Dylan is God.*"

A half-hour later I drove into the town of Clermont l'Hérault, mentally drained and weak with hunger. It was now almost nine o'clock in the evening, and I had neither eaten nor found a hotel for the night. In a word, I was vulnerable. And with predictable inevitability, there suddenly loomed from the roadside in front of me not the *Logis de France* I yearned for but a pair of golden arches—the gleaming, ubiquitous ***M***.

McDonald's had made its beachhead in France at least a quarter of a century earlier—I remembered my cuisine-weary sons dragging me into one in Paris back in the late 70's—and with every subsequent trip to the country I'd seen a few more. But aside from occasional emergency toilet stops—their single saving grace, from my vantage point, despite the fact you now had to pay to use them—I hadn't set foot inside the garish portals ever since. No corporate force other than Wal-Mart had laid greater waste to my own nation's rural culture, a gnawing fact even my hunger pangs couldn't fully suppress. Slowing the car to a stop, I sat parked on the shoulder as my stomach and my conscience waged internecine war.

A bag of fast food would have shamed me anywhere in France, but mere hours after accepting a forty-dollar gift bottle of wine from a man so principled even the skeptical Pius had called him a local hero, I knew it would feel like a craven betrayal of Judas proportions. On the other hand, my gut responded, much as Huck Finn's had whenever he wrestled with his conscience, there were at least a couple of extenuating circumstances, take it all around. The first was the fact I still didn't have a room for the night and might conceivably be forced, if I didn't eat soon, to spend it on an empty stomach. The second, which cut even closer to the bone, had been bred into my genes by a Scottish mother who dismissed her occasional splurges on clothes and jewelry as "rare bargains" only a fool would have passed up. A French McDonald's was a chance to do sociological research, the devil in my gut whispered—an opportunity to scout behind enemy lines. Stifling my scruples, I crept on toward the brightly lit building and pulled in.

Whether the next quarter of an hour was the day's apex or nadir is open to question, but it was unmistakably the most surreal, like drifting through an art gallery and arriving at a *trompe-l'œil* painting that stops you dead in your tracks. You think you know exactly what you're staring at, when the ground abruptly falls away under your feet. As in America, nearly everyone in this Franco-McDonald's was young—both the eaters and the workers—and the building had the familiar profit-maxing corporate sterility right down to the kiddie-seducing posters plugging spin-off action heroes on the walls. The *carte* too trumpeted all the usual fare in English, or at least in that McDonaldese esperanto that's become even more universal. Hamburgers, cheeseburgers, Big Macs and Chicken McNuggets. If my devil's bargain hadn't forced my eyes further down the menu, I might have fled the place with my sack of food and the brief delusion that I'd just pulled in off I-80 back in the States.

There was no hurrying the young woman behind the counter, though, which is where the floor began to fall away. I was second in line. The baseball-capped young father ahead of me, after twice scurrying back to a booth to consult with his wife and three kids for confirmation, placed his order in French. "*Cinq chaize burgaires. Deux cheeken MacNoogets. Une Croque Mac-Do. Deux Mac-Creespies et un Cornet de Dessert Glace. Aussi, trois Mac-Flooreez et deux bières.*" The family was sitting under a "*Zone fumeurs*" sign and the wife was puffing a cigarette. A larger sign next to it read "*Vous allez Fondre pour Son Craquant!*" Using my pocket dictionary, I translated it as "You are going to be lightning-struck by your Crackling Thing," though the print was hard to read through the glaze that had formed over my eyes.

The server handed the scribbled order to the nearest of three other young workers in the kitchen, one of whom stood idly by, stifling a yawn. Turning back to the counter, the server took out her pad again and scribbled several orders more. The line behind me was now three or four deep, and we stood silently watching as she began frenetically wrapping and bagging items, making the three MacFlurries, and scooping half a dozen orders of *frites* into paper bags. The yawning worker in the kitchen finally shuffled out to wrap a single burger, then just as inexplicably returned to her idling post in the rear. My own order was as simple as an order gets—two cheeseburgers and a box of McNuggets—but I stood waiting as the clock on the wall ticked off minute after creeping minute. No one in the line behind me complained; all of us simply stood there watching. When I finally received my bag and skulked back to my car, easily fifteen minutes had passed.

Settled at last in a local hotel room a half-hour later, I lay on the bed wolfing down the artery-clogging food and reflecting on the bizarre experience. Whatever its commercial success, the attempt to graft American production values on French roots seemed to me a colossal cultural failure. I had unfortunately not been able to sample the fare at *Au Pressoir*, the little restaurant back in Saint Saturnin, but I had little doubt I'd have risen from the table both well nourished and free of the hunger pangs that remained largely unsated even as the last McNugget slid down my throat. Yet Pius had told me the restaurant was losing money. I longed for a reverse influence—the grafting of French rural culture on my own native land.

In the end, I knew the cultural tide would continue to run in the direction it had long been running—that *Titanic* was the all-time box-office film in France, the person the French had Googled most often the year before was Britney Spears, and *Le Texas Burger* had recently been a smash hit at a McDonald's in Paris. What I did not yet know was that the influx of land-buying invaders flooding the Hérault valley would soon include many more English and increasing numbers of Americans far less exotic than COYOTE's founder, drawn by the falling price of vineyards in the wake of *la crise*. My evening audience with the bohemian pope had fortunately left a few matters unexplored, including his views on how my country's culture was impacting the one he inhabited. I was silently relieved he'd cut me off before I could pursue them. He had his own America, and for a moment in time at least, I still had my France.

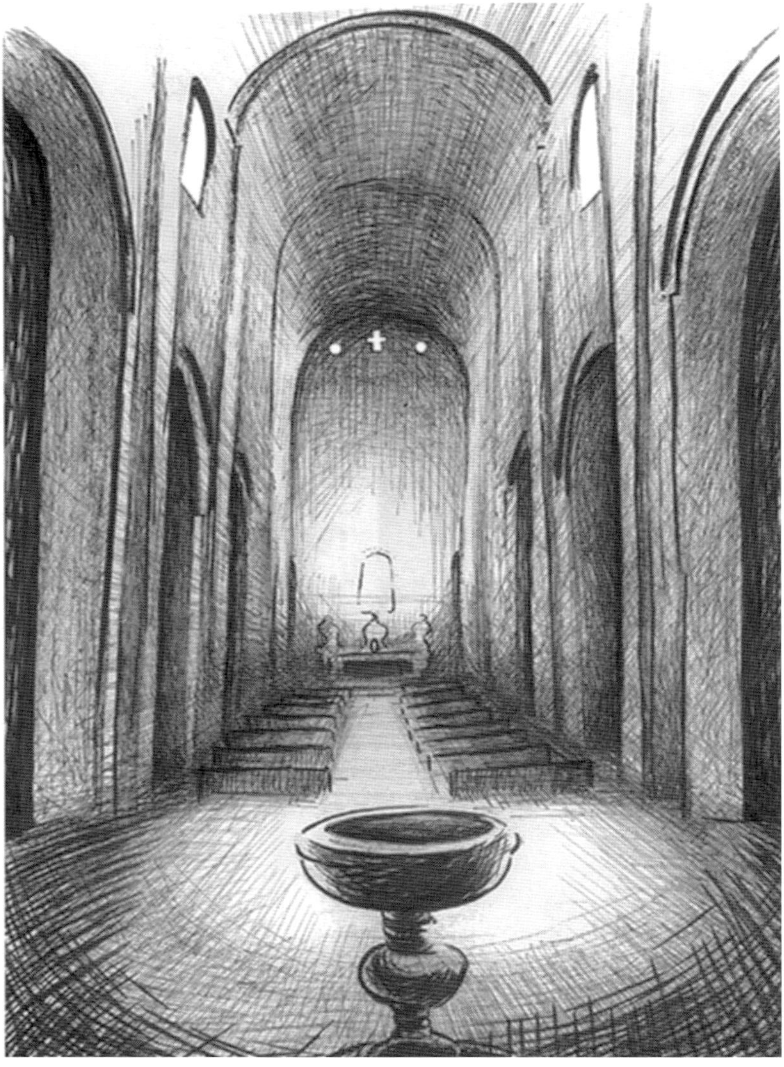

Chapter 9
Digestif

"*Gardez la sacoche.*"

The warning had come years before, in the most casual of after-dinner conversations, but I'd reached the point in my trip where I knew I couldn't avoid its implications any longer. Still, I lingered in Clermont L'Hérault as I'd lingered in Sète a week earlier, acutely aware that my next destination threatened to shadow, if anything could, the glowing image I'd so long held of rural France.

It was the kind of memory you try to suppress. Relaxing in a small restaurant in another village an hour from Monteyroux during the sabbatical period Jane and I had lived there, we were lingering over dessert and coffee when the owner approached our table holding a bottle of amber liquid in his hand. We'd had affable snatches of conversation with him throughout the evening, and the room had emptied except for the three of us. Uncorking the bottle, he sat down next to us and poured two complimentary shots of the *digestif*. It had a bite that tasted unmistakably of thyme.

We both thanked him and commented on the distinctive flavor. Yes, he said, he had made it—gathered the herbs himself in the hills outside the village. He poured himself a glass and we chatted on in French, warmed by the alcohol and the pleasure that comes from briefly surmounting a language barrier, however mundane the subject at hand. Ours moved from the piquant drink to other *boissons* and foods native to the region; the rugged beauty of the uplands; places we'd already been and others we hoped to visit during the remainder of our stay. One of them was a nearby town called Lodève.

A frown clouded his face at the name and he shook his head. No, he said, don't go there. If you do you risk having your car broken into. "*Beaucoup de Musulmans,*" he lowered his voice to a whisper, bending toward us in exaggerated concern. I don't recall the exact phrase he used next, only that it was a rough French equivalent of our "wetbacks" or "camel jockeys." Lodève was filled with Muslims, he repeated, his hand dropping theatrically to his hip pocket. If you go there, "*gardez la sacoche*," he cautioned. Protect your wallet. They'll steal everything they can.

I had grown up with ethnic prejudice. Its presence in the prairie villages of my childhood was as unremarked, and instinctive, as breathing the corn-pollinated air. Most of it was more a cultural reflex than actively malicious—casual references to "jewing down" a car dealer or the "niggertoes" in a Christmas basket of mixed nuts. It was not until high school that I came face to face with the more virulent variety. As a five-foot-two-inch freshman who rarely got off the bench, I had somehow managed to stick on the basketball varsity and was included in the three-car caravan that ferried the team to games away from home. My first such trip came in the flashy red Thunderbird of our hip, crew-cut young coach, a former minor league baseball player every boy in the school idolized. Squeezed into the back seat between two cackling senior starters, I listened in a wide-eyed daze to his profane riffs on "all the fucking jigaboos" and "jungle bunnies" he'd had to play with in the minors—the "night fighters" that had taken over the sport once the color barrier went down.

That experience, and others like it, had been my introduction to the darker side of small-town life in America. And while the French restaurant owner's bigoted comments had poisoned a previously delightful evening, I was far more repelled than stunned that his *digestif* had loosed a racist tongue. Ignoring his warnings, Jane and I spent the next afternoon in Lodève, predictably without incident, even though we parked our car on a street where the Muslim presence was clear.

But the sour taste had lingered. His xenophobic slurs had opened religious and ethnic fault lines beneath the placid surface of the French campagne too deep to ignore, and the memory returned whenever I saw a North African man or a shawled woman. Close to six million Muslims lived in France, nearly a tenth of the total population, an increasing number of them unemployed youths who had reportedly grown so angry and disillusioned they approved of Islamist jihads. The tensions had been heightened further by a recent national law banning the wearing of any "ostensibly religious" symbol in French public schools—a contentious, maybe even desperate measure to preserve the church/state separation the acerbic dog-walker back in Cahors had told me was the best thing his country had ever accomplished, a country that had endured some of history's bloodiest religious wars. Most French Christians and Jews were apparently in favor of *la loi contre le voile*—"the law against the veil" as it had come to be known—but a number of resident Muslims were demanding that their religion be taught in the nation's classrooms. The tensions hit painfully close to home the longer I considered them. My own homeland was rife with similar post-9/11 anxiety, a fact that registered with shaming force every time I glanced uneasily at my fellow passengers waiting to board an airplane. And the aggressive agendas of Christian evangelicals and other political pressure groups increasingly threatened the last vestiges of communal inclusiveness as a democratic ideal. All of it conspired to make Lodève the most problematic stop of my trip.

I made a last, nostalgic visit before returning to it—drove back through the gray-walled gorge of the upper Hérault to St. Guilhem le Désert.

Sacred to relic-venerating Christians for over a millennium, the site had been celebrated as far back as the twelfth century in a pilgrimage guide to Santiago de Compostela, on the west coast of Spain. Though its incomparable cloisters now graced a sylvan space in New York City, the ancient abbey church still stood where it had been built all those violent centuries ago, wedged at the top of a narrow canyon above a trickling spring. I wanted to make the climb up to it again for several reasons, one of them the memory of the last time I'd stood in the sanctuary, more than ten years before.

It had been awhile since I'd worshipped in a church, even back then, and the veneration of relics had always struck my Protestant eyes as naive superstition. But the quiet faith that moved people to profound depths of sacrifice and devotion was a different matter.

Just outside Cortona during our idyll in Bramasole, Jane and I had stared in awe at the ascetic cell of Francis of Assisi, his bed a slab of stone no wider than a bookshelf; my academic career as a medievalist had centered on Chaucer's *Canterbury Tales*, whose opening lines remained a heart-stirring evocation of the spiritual healing that was any true pilgrimage's loftiest goal. There were *fatwa*-and-Scripture-bellowing zealots, in short, and there were saints. What I knew of the historical Count Guillaume—or *Guilhem* as he was called in the language of Oc—suggested that he had earned his assigned place among the latter. The purported sliver of Christ's cross that was his little church's most hallowed possession had been given to the warrior hero when he'd stopped battling infidels and withdrawn to the remote site to build an abbey. The donor was Charlemagne, his overlord, who had brought the relic back from Jerusalem. So at least countless numbers of the faithful had believed since the early ninth century. Their pilgrimages, sometimes from hundreds of miles distant, were made to venerate both the priceless artifact and the saint's preserved bones.

Jane and I had made our own trek up to the abbey church from Montpeyroux on that spring morning a decade earlier—gazed dutifully at the dusty relics in their bejeweled reliquaries and felt only the historical interest a pair of academics would naturally feel. Eventually she'd returned to the square, lured by its sun-dappled tables under the spreading boughs of the region's oldest and most impressive plain tree. I whispered that I'd join her in a few minutes and remained in the sanctuary, content to idle a bit longer inside its austere walls.

How does one explain a fleeting moment that feels suddenly, almost painfully spiritual? At the far end of the nave, candles flickered below the reliquaries. A shaft of sunlight filtered through a cross-shaped aperture in the stone above the altar. As I stood there, alone and silent, it pierced the church's dim interior like a celestial arrow to the heart. The feeling was similar to what I'd felt at Chartres, gazing up at the cathedral's west portal in the moonlight—similar even to moments I'd occasionally experienced on some wondrously limpid trout stream. I didn't attempt to analyze it further, simply remained there watching the play of sunlight dance and finally dissolve on the worn stone floor the muffled feet of generations had trod before my own. At some point my mind registered that it was April, the month Chaucer's pilgrims had set off for Canterbury. Mystical or sentimental, the moment had left *St. Guilhem le Désert* firmly impressed on my soul.

The parking lot at its base was empty when I arrived. Zipping my jacket tight against the winter chill, I trudged the winding road up to the shrine, encountering no one until I reached the stone square. An old man sat on a bench under the leafless plane tree, bent over a cane in his gnarled hands. I nodded to him as I passed and walked on into the church, it too empty of other visitors. This time my experience in the nave was simply a prolonged, quiet pleasure. When I left a half hour later, the old man was gone, the *place* vacant. I spent another few minutes on the bench he'd abandoned, admiring the ancient square, then started back down the hill to my car.

I'd walked perhaps a hundred yards when I met a middle-aged man carrying a fresh baguette, his head sheathed in a thin blue stocking cap. His cheeks were rosy from the cold. A small cut had been recently medicated on his chin.

We bid each other the obligatory *bonjours* as we approached, and on an impulse I shuffled to a stop, pleased when he smiled and stopped as well. His obvious friendliness carried the bonus of a good, if painstakingly measured command of English, and we were soon chatting comfortably in the street. It was clear he was both intelligent and uncommonly reflective, his halting speech a mark of the careful thought he'd given to the larger world beyond the pilgrimage site.

His name was Yann, he said, which by coincidence was the same as the laconic youth's I'd met in Souillac two weeks earlier. He had been a doctor in another part of the country, he told me, but now lived in St. Guilhem le Désert. Glancing back up the hill at the abbey church, I asked if he was religious. Yes, he said, quite religious. And yes, he added as our conversation deepened, what was happening throughout the world in the name of religion was an appalling thing.

I asked him what he thought of the recent Presidential election in America—whether he had any feelings about the role religion had played in it. He paused at least ten seconds before answering. "The fate of the world makes Bush president," he said finally. "Not Bush who has made the state of the world." The comment seemed penetrating—and cryptic—enough I too said nothing for some time, simply nodded and waited for him to go on.

"It is the system of... of...." He looked away, toward the snow-crusted cliff above us, searching for the word. "Of *consumption*," he continued, finding it. "That is the real problem."

He saw that I remained uncertain of his meaning, and went on. "The *fanatique* is not religious," he said. "It is caricature. It is idolatry. The fault with *fanatisme* is a confusion between true religion and...." He stopped again, searching for the right word. "And *méthodologie*," he finally said in French. "Idolatry—*Musulman, Chrétien*—it is a very big problem. The confusion in the world is everywhere now."

I told him religious extremism—*fanatisme*—didn't seem as pronounced in France. Was I right, or had I missed something?

"The religious *fanatisme* is an... an *écho*...." Not sure if the word existed in English, he made a hollow hooting sound, cupping his mouth, as I nodded. "An echo of economic *fanatisme*" he went on. "The occidental society makes the *fanatisme économique*. Production, production, production. Consumerism. It is form of *fanatisme*. All *fanatismes*... of the ego—'Look at me! Look at me!'"—he pointed to his chest in a pantomime of narcissism—"it is the same process. Every integrate of *fanatisme* meet...meet... meets? (I nodded) the other forms because there is no... no... no *sagacité*," he fell back on French. "No *lucidité*, no...*wisdom*," he finally hit on the English word he'd been searching for. "What to do different I do not know. But one thing sure. The process individual"—another long pause—"I don't see a solution if the man, the woman, live individually. They must develop more *sagacité* of their own lives. There are many people who don't *appliquent* the things they say."

The conversation had lasted perhaps fifteen minutes but left me with much to chew on as I walked on down the hill. The verb, unfortunately, was entirely metaphorical. Though it was barely noon, the sweet-smelling loaf of bread in the doctor's gloved hand had left me almost as hungry as I'd been before my brief apostasy at the golden arches a few days before. On the walk up, I'd passed a small metal sign creaking in the wind, "*pizza à emporter*" painted on the swinging panel. Pausing only to glance at the *carte* beside the doorway, I ducked in.

A rawboned woman with dyed blonde hair sat at a wooden table by the counter, reading a newspaper and puffing a cigarette through remarkably bad teeth. But she was as friendly as the cerebral physician, shooing me back outside with an indulgent laugh for a longer look at the menu in the window when I hesitated over the half dozen pizza options she gave. I quickly made my selection and returned. While her husband prepared the food in the kitchen, I took advantage of her obvious good nature and raised some of the questions the doctor had left unresolved in my mind. She didn't appear to hold it against me when I confirmed that I was an American, though "*Boosh*"—she rasped the word disgustedly, shaking her head through the smoke—was "*dangereux, pour le monde entier.*"

America had "*une grande importance dans le monde,*" she continued, taking another deep drag. You had "*un bon Président,*" she assured me. "*Mais maintenant, Boosh.*" But now, Bush. Half the voters in America would have shared my sardonic grunt at the words. She shook her head again, then laughed derisively as the smoke rattled in her throat. "*Monique Lewinskay,*" she rasped, rolling her eyes with a disdain that said such a farcical escapade could never have brought down a President of France. "*Vous êtes trop....*" She hesitated, not as the physician had paused, groping for the right word, but visibly not wanting to offend me. Apparently satisfied that I understood she was talking about my country and not my personal habits, she finished the sentence. "*Vous êtes trop puritains,*" she said—too puritan.

Nodding, I asked her whether she saw any of that same puritanical zeal in France. "*Non,*" she answered emphatically. "*Pas du tout.*" We are "*beaucoup plus libres,*" she added. In *la France*, there was "*beaucoup plus de tolerance.*"

It seemed a relevant time to raise again the delicate issue that had occupied my thoughts all morning, the Muslim presence in Lodève. The woman shook her head again. No, she said, there wasn't any problem. They had come from *Algérie* decades ago and settled into the community. They were not *fanatiques*. "*Non non non non non,*" she repeated, though I'd said nothing to challenge her—"*Priorité, allier avec la France pendant la guerre.*" They had been "*obligés de partir de autres Musulmans*"— compelled to leave other Muslims back in Algeria and ally with France during the war.

Her husband emerged from the kitchen holding the boxed pizza at that point, and I ventured only a couple of questions more. Are you religious, I asked as politely as I could. Both of them nodded, and the woman added an emphatic "*Oui. Très religieuse.*" I told them how much I admired the quiet beauty of the village's ancient church—asked if its crucifixion relic was important to them. "*Absolument,*" the husband responded solemnly. The woman was more expansive. That it was "*authentique*" there could be no doubt, she assured me. Charlemagne himself had testified to it. And the church was indeed very beautiful. If only its cloisters hadn't been sold to Rockefeller—she rubbed her fingers together in the universal symbol of avarice—it would be even more "*magnifique.*" But such a thing could not happen now, she added more cheerfully. "*Il n'y a plus de possibilité. C'est fini.*"

I drove across the narrow stone bridge into Lodève an hour later. At first glance the town looked more prosperous than I remembered it, so much so that I drove for several blocks through its bustling center before finding a place to park. The Muslim presence was everywhere apparent, though of several black-clad women in hijabs I saw none wearing the niqab, the full face covering broken only by a narrow slit revealing the eyes. My recent conversations with Monsieur Guibert in Aniane and the keen-eyed restaurateur Pius had both reinforced what the pizza woman had stated so unequivocally. There was no significant ethnic conflict in the region, even in this larger, religiously mixed town of six thousand. There had been some problems in the past, all of them acknowledged, but things were a lot better now.

I didn't distrust them, but in light of what I'd recently read about the volatile tensions elsewhere in France I wanted to withhold judgment until I'd spoken with at least one or two of the town's residents. The *mairie*, or city hall, was just across the large square where I'd parked, and I decided a good place to start would be with an official response to the awkward questions I still carried from that evening with the racist restaurant owner ten years before.

A taciturn secretary behind the front desk sized me up for several seconds, then stiffly directed me up an impressive staircase to a large room on the third floor, the file-cluttered office of the man she'd told me was *"Le Politique de la Ville."* I paused outside to look up the honorific in my pocket dictionary and found only "politician." The room was empty when I walked through the open doorway, but its occupant soon emerged from down the hall. A gregarious, heavy-set man in his thirties, he soon seemed satisfied that my intentions weren't hostile and invited me to sit down. His job had many duties, he said in French—education, prevention of "*bêtises*" or stupidity in the community, social and economic development, "*etcetera etcetera.*" Yes, he confirmed, Lodève had a significant Muslim population—almost twenty percent of its residents. Some of the youngest were third-generation French, and they and their families had made good lives in the town. There were no serious tensions. If I could return on Friday and speak with his Muslim assistant, he felt sure Djibali would tell me the same thing. *La loi contre le voile* hadn't caused any problem in the local schools because no girl wanted to wear one. The more extreme examples of Islamist fundamentalism—female genital mutilation, for example—were unheard of. That there were absolutely no jihadist sympathizers in Lodève he had no way of knowing for sure, he ended, but it was a very tiny and isolated minority if there were.

He struck me as both honest and objective, as objective at least as a public official can be dealing with issues as sensitive as those I'd raised. Thanking him, I said I was genuinely sorry to have missed the chance to speak with his Muslim assistant, but didn't doubt that his perspective would have been much the same as his own.

Uncertain where to turn next, I considered simply letting the matter drop and taking at face value the upbeat view of things I'd gotten from everyone I'd met. My near non-existent gaucherie threshold notwithstanding, I hadn't quite reached the point of stopping one of the several black-shawled women I passed on the street to ask if genital mutilation was ever practiced in Lodève. Settling instead for a cup of coffee, I walked back across the square to a small brasserie near my car. Several people sat quietly eating or sipping beer at a set of well-worn tables, and it was some time before the busy waiter, the only visible employee in the place, got to mine. A lithe, doe-eyed young man with jet-dark hair and a dusky complexion that suggested family roots in North Africa, he was also the age when idealistic fervor runs highest. Over the coffee and an excellent *salade niçoise*, I spent the next half-hour contemplating the cross-cultural implications of telling him why I'd come to his town and asking for his help.

When I finally worked up the nerve and did so, he told me he was nineteen, his name was Benchabane, and yes, he was Muslim. He went to the local *mosquée* every Friday and prayed in his house the other six days of the week. I told him that I was an American. That my wife and I had spent a few weeks near Lodève ten years earlier, and I knew there had been some ethnic and religious tensions in the region back then. Would he feel comfortable answering a few questions, from his vantage point as a Muslim, on the situation now?

However delicately I framed it, such a question from a total stranger bordered on the invasive, maybe even the boorish, and I wouldn't have blamed him if he'd responded with the lip-curling scorn the stereotypical French are infamous for. Instead he nodded and agreed immediately. If I could return at three, he said, he should be far less busy and we could talk then.

I passed the next couple of hours walking around the town and noting the numerous ways in which it appeared to reinforce the official view the *Politique de la Ville* had given me. A shawled woman shared a laugh with a blond fruit vendor as she bought a bag of oranges. Two Muslim girls in jeans and tastefully applied makeup checked out the latest fashions in a corner boutique. I walked back to the café at the appointed hour and took out my pen, notebook, and portable tape recorder as Benchabane served dessert to a couple at the last occupied table, then sat down opposite my chair.

Over the next hour, two or three other people entered and required his attentions, but for the most part we sat quietly talking—a young French Muslim and a probing foreigner from the country that had become the most hated on the planet to many of his faith. Acutely aware of the fact, I asked him about this yawning divide between the Islamic world and my own.

It was because of the difference between what people had and what they needed, he responded. They were trying to construct "*un autre monde*"—another world—because of the poverty. It was bad but understandable—inevitable—the kind of thing that would always happen when people with the same basic values but different levels of income, and different religions, reached a crisis point.

I asked how he felt about Al Qaeda, Bin Laden, terrorist jihads.

This too was very bad, he said—all of it—but a way of life. If their fathers admired it—their brothers—they followed it. And because of that, if they were poor and saw no hope for the future, there was no reasoning. "*Pas de rationalité.*"

Were there any terrorist sympathizers in Lodève, I risked.

He paused for some time before responding.

"*Peut-être quelques personnes,*" he answered softly—maybe a few, "*pas beaucoup.*" Only the young men, he added, peering deep into my eyes. "*Seulement des jeunes.*"

Would it become a bigger problem?

"*Oui,*" he nodded. "*Sans doute.*" Support was becoming more and more popular. The big problem was the *chômage*, he added—the unemployment. Not so much in places like Lodève but in the bigger cities, Paris especially. He himself was fine, he said when I asked about his own economic future. His father had started the café twelve years earlier and he enjoyed working there.

I asked him about the controversial "*loi contre la voile.*" What had been its effects in Lodève?

Some prohibited articles were still worn, he answered, but now students had to hide them. (Among the "*ostensiblement religieuse*" items the government had banned were skullcaps, turbans, and large crosses.) People would gradually turn away from religion because they weren't allowed to express it, he said. Life became too difficult. There were *"plus de pièges"*—more traps. The police asked you why you were driving the way you were. Still, he went on, it was a part of democracy. It kept people from what was worse, political hatred. Kept them from becoming victims, and that was a good thing.

In general, I asked, how would he describe the life of Muslims in Lodève.

It was better than in the cities, he repeated. Most people had work, and the society was more open. *"La société est plus ouverte."* Christians and Muslims even married each other. This was not uncommon. His brother had married a Christian woman three years before.

He paused, smiling shyly, then added that his own girlfriend was a Christian as well.

For a nineteen-year-old who had lived all his life in a small provincial town and had only a high school education, he struck me as remarkably well-informed and thoughtful, and I ventured a couple of final questions about my own troubled land.

Most people in my country didn't know a lot about France, I confessed, and I was curious. Did he have a very clear image of the U.S.?

We understand America here mostly from the television, he replied. And it was *peut-être* not always accurate. But I think America is killing itself, he added, lowering his eyes. *"L'Amérique se tue elle-même."* Everything was for the money—for the petrol. And for Israel.

It was a war inside the head, he continued, looking up at me and pointing a finger at his temple. *"La guerre dans la tête."* We were shocked here when Bush won, he said, adding his own voice to what seemed a nearly universal reaction throughout his country. I think it was a result of the economy, he added tentatively. The poor people turn to their religion to make themselves feel better, *non?*

A school teacher I'd sat next to at a seafood restaurant in Sète had told me that every *lycée* student in France who earned a diploma—"*le bac*" as the equivalent of our high school degree was called colloquially—was required to take three years of philosophy. Staring across the table at the nineteen-year-old waiter, whose formal education remained unknown to me, I found the claim very easy to believe.

I left Lodève a short time later but found my thoughts returning to the youth often in the following months. His ominous words about the inevitable consequences of poverty and hopelessness took on a prophetic grimness when the firestorm of rioting swept the dead-end *banlieues* of Paris and other cities later in the summer, as they did again, less than a year after we'd sat quietly talking, when the protests against the government's draconian proposals on unemployment swelled to half a million people marching under the banner "*Non à l'insécurité.*" As in May of 1968, France's universities would be the flashpoint of the strikes and scattered acts of violence televised to the world through clouds of tear gas, the streets around the Sorbonne filled once more with angry students marching for a cause. Watching it all from the safe remove of my cabin retreat in the woods, back home in Minnesota, I thought of a young French Muslim who had surely never been there, but just as surely understood.

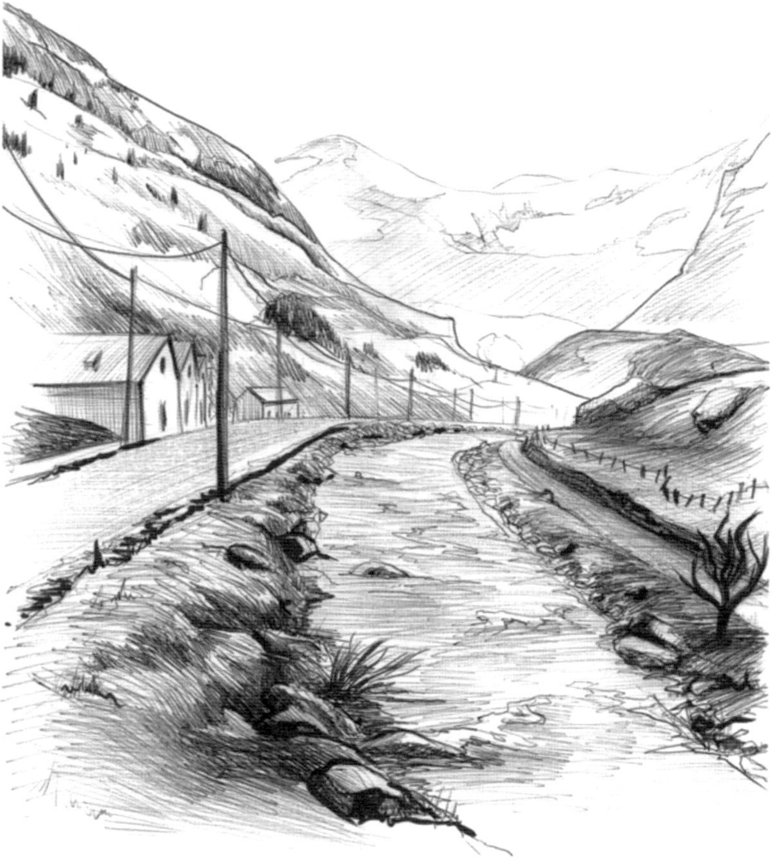

Chapter 10
Frogs

One last, whimsical trip objective remained. Somewhere on a hilltop in Burgundy there was a place too tiny even to be called a village—a half dozen scattered buildings with a quaint, three-*chambre* hotel owned by an aging couple named Monique and Daniel. The pair had an English sheepdog that was almost as long in the tooth in dog years, a big, friendly mutt with hair covering his eyes and a fondness for lying on your feet as you lingered over Monique's terrific *coq au vin*. His name was *Goudou*, and he spoke fluent, forgiving hound regardless of how you pronounced it. The version I favored hearkened back to the farm dogs of my boyhood, which his slobbery, foot-licking indolence recalled. Southern Nebraska wasn't quite the Ozarks, but it was within hailing distance, and despite Jane's grimaces I couldn't resist scratching his hairy back and tossing him an occasional scrap under the table, cooing "*Gooooo-dooooooo. You a good dog, you.*"

In the mind's eye, it was the perfect place to spend the last couple of nights of a tour through provincial France before my return to Paris. The challenge was finding it again, since I recalled neither the site's name nor the exact part of Burgundy where Jane and I and our two sometime traveling companions the Johnsons had stumbled on it six years before. I also wasn't sure, even if I could locate the remote little hotel, that it stayed open during the winter. Neither complication troubled me greatly. There were countless other inns in Burgundy nearly as tempting. If I had to forego Goudou's company on this trip, *c'est la vie*.

My attitude in general had become just as free-wheeling, in the way travel moods can when you realize only days remain before your return to the mundane realities of home. I had few illusions that the trip had plumbed the depths of *la France profonde*. But my fondness for the country had survived the closest soundings I could register. The contacts with people who would soon be both busier and more guarded under the summer influx of tourists had combined with the prolonged severity of the weather to make the trip feel different from any other I'd previously taken, the way it felt to suddenly find yourself standing inside the home of a person you'd politely nodded to for years passing on the street.

With nearly a week to kill before my flight out of Paris, deciding on a route from Languedoc back to the city thus offered that delicious traveler's luxury of sacrificing planning to whim. The morning after I left Lodève, rolling north on the autoroute, the first one registered at 130 kilometers an hour—a roadside sign with an abstract picture of a bridge above the name "*Millau*."

The image did what the city's name alone hadn't done when I'd looked briefly at my map a night earlier—jogged the memory of a recently completed work of architecture reputed to be among the glories of the world. The French had dubbed it simply "*Le Viaduc de Millau*." Turning off at the next exit, I spiraled down a series of switch-back curves into a deep gorge where other signs soon confirmed it. A view of the *Viaduc* lay just ahead.

I had never seen a bridge that struck the same chords of emotion the Golden Gate stirred in me whenever it first came into sight on trips to San Francisco. But the French bridge came close. I rounded a bend and there it suddenly was, still miles ahead but almost palpably in front of me, like some luminous white feather fletched with gossamer against the gun-metal sky. I pulled off the road and sat for several minutes, gaping at it, then drove on to another turn-out and gaped some more. It took close to an hour to reach the valley floor and funnel my way through the congested little city, then drive the several kilometers on until the span soared hundreds of feet directly above my head.

I was now on a narrow, virtually untraveled country road. Creeping down it, I searched for an access sign pointing the way back up to the *viaduc*—the autoroute flowing on toward Paris over the ethereal structure I learned later was the tallest traffic bridge in the world.

Lying at the confluence of two deep gorges, Millau had experienced for decades some of the worst traffic jams in French history, and the bridge's renowned architect, Sir Norman Foster, had aptly likened the liberating arc across the valley to "flying a car." I knew none of this at the time, nor that in 1999 Millau had also briefly caught the world's attention when an anti-globalization activist named José Bove led a group of protesters who demolished a half-built McDonald's near his sheep farm. On that wintry morning, I knew only that the views of the bridge had been breathtaking, but the way back up to it was nowhere to be seen.

Retracing my course through the city bottleneck seemed to be the only, acutely unappealing option, yet I was on the verge of doing so as I crept a few hundred aimless yards farther up the valley, where another roadside sign appeared. This one was hand-painted, barely larger than a dinner plate. *Roquefort*, it read. *18 km.* The sign triggered a decision as instantaneous as my descent to the bridge. "*Roquefort*" might well have been the first spoken word of French I had ever heard, falling from my mother's lips at some roadside diner back in the 1940's. I had no way of knowing for sure, since I'd have been a babe in arms when she uttered it. I knew only that a good Wisconsin cheddar remained one of her favorite foods, and the celebrated French variety—in Cornhusker-speak either "*Rock-a-fort*" or "that stinky stuff? I don't know how anybody can stomach it"—lay somewhere down in the gastronomic netherlands with tripe, brains, and head cheese.

Thoughts of the latter trio continued to turn my own stomach. That much at least of her insular prairie genes ran deep in my veins. But by the time I'd reached graduate school, the pungent French *fromage* had risen so high on my own personal list of favored comestibles I boycotted restaurants where I couldn't get it on a dinner salad. That may seem difficult to believe now—if not my level of obsession, which has probably become all too conceivable, the fact that Roquefort dressing was commonly available in rural Nebraska, and called by that name. But it was, at least back then, in the middle of the last century. If I'd been born a few decades later, "blue cheese" would undoubtedly have been the derisive words my infant ears picked up from my mother's lips.

Whenever my first exposure, the crude sign pointing to *Roquefort* barely ten miles away made the decision a no-brainer. All thought of the autoroute forgotten, I drove on up the obscure canyon road taking a perverse pleasure in the knowledge that had Jane and the Johnsons been with me, Yvonne Johnson, at least, would have understood. She liked Roquefort dressing as much as I did. A few months earlier, after an overpriced dinner in a chichi restaurant in Minneapolis, we'd mutually threatened to start carrying secreted stashes of the stuff as an alternative to the dreaded vinaigrette.

If it's true that one sin breeds another, the same is surely true of impulse. My next spontaneous decision came only a few kilometers farther up the road. A purling little stream had emerged on my left, its ice-fringed waters dancing over riffles and runs as clear as crystal. It had been almost half a year since I'd cast a trout fly. The portable little rod I'd brought for just such a serendipitous opportunity remained stowed away in the trunk. Braking to a stop to eye the water more closely, I sat parked on the deserted highway for half a minute, then pulled over on the shoulder and switched off the engine. Changing into a pair of jeans and spare set of running shoes, I added a sweater under my jacket against the sub-freezing temperatures and descended the rocky bank to the brook.

I'd like to report that the ensuing hour's quest for the wild *truit* of Roquefort turned out to be as rewarding as my hunt for *les truffes* a few days earlier. The truth is that I fished a half-mile of frigid, knee-deep water without a strike. Shivering uncontrollably, I returned to the car in that state of manic euphoria shared by lunatics and compulsive anglers. I stopped fishing only because it had begun to snow and become numbingly clear the winter water was still too cold for trout to be active, as Pierre Affre had assured me it would be during our chat in Paris. None of it mattered. I would have released anything I caught regardless. Shucking the soaked clothes off my goose-pimpled flesh and rifling my suitcase for three dry layers, I rolled jauntily on up the road with the car's heater blasting and *contrast value* firmly restored as life's most profound truth.

The tiny village I'd fixed on, perched scenically near the top of a *mont* three switchback kilometers above the stream, appeared no more active than the fish when I reached it fifteen minutes later and crept on up its narrow main street. There was no hotel in sight. The scattered handful of shops and shuttered houses were closed as tight as the mouths of the trout had been. Yet half a dozen signs confirmed that somewhere in the village I would find its world-renowned product, which as far back as the eighteenth-century the French encyclopedist Diderot had called "*le roi des fromages.*" (Only later did I learn that numerous other French villages were named Roquefort. I'd simply stumbled on the celebrated one). Parking the car, I walked on up the steeply pitched street and finally arrived at a building that was open—a cheese factory. A young woman sat dutifully behind a desk just inside the entrance, and she greeted me with the sunny zeal of a caffeine-juiced telemarketer. A guided tour of the caves would begin in twenty minutes, she informed me brightly, and would reveal the miracle of the cheesemaking process from beginning to end. It promised to be the kind of mind-glazing indoctrination a canny traveler learns to flee like bed lice, but her glowing description of the divine tastes I was about to experience momentarily wore my defenses down. The *Viaduc* had taken my breath away, as had the impulsive hour on the trout stream, if only from its groin-numbing temperatures. Figuring I was playing with the house's money, I decided to go for the trifecta, and laid my three euros down.

The house won. Ticket in hand, I shuffled off with half a dozen other dazed pilgrims through the longest sixty minutes I'd experienced since my last colonoscopy.

Our guide was another irrepressible young woman, who appeared even more dedicated to her work than the one at the door. Leading us down into the subterranean network of bone-chilling chambers that underlay the village, she paused every few feet to tell us more about the making, aging, and history of the illustrious *fromage* than all but the most addicted cheese aficionado could ever hope to know. And that was only the first fifteen minutes. Our subsequent stops included a series of creaking sound & light shows that might have been rigged by some wizened techno-junkie stoned on LSD. Maybe I'd have been more receptive if I'd always wanted to learn the cell structure of ewe's milk. Or if I'd had the foresight to wrap my still shivering flesh in a fourth layer of dry clothes. Or maybe not, it's hard to say. I did learn that Casanova used Roquefort cheese to seduce women, a fact that, had I known it back in my salad days, would have put an entirely different spin on the question of whether to stash a vial of my favorite dressing in my pants.

The tour predictably ended in a glossy salesroom, where neatly toothpicked samples had been strategically set out for us in front of several gleaming, refrigerated cases filled with the company's three varieties of the cheese. All were nearly as tasty as promised, but in an uncharacteristic moment of restraint, I kept my wallet in my pocket. Whatever my fellow pilgrims' decision, I hadn't climbed the hallowed mountain for cheese processed in a factory. Following the *sortie* signs down a long tunnel, I was suddenly disgorged a few yards from my car.

Just across the street, a weathered sign above a padlocked door read "*Le Vieux Berger, Artisan Fromager.*" The hole-in-the-wall shop looked like it might have been closed for decades, but a woman passing on the sidewalk assured me it would open again, as always, in the spring. The owner, she said, lived just outside the village, higher up *le mont*. I found the place fifteen minutes later. There weren't any visible sheep on the property, and the Old Shepherd who answered my knock wore a natty black turtleneck and looked to be around thirty years old. But the blue-veined chunk of cheese I bought from him felt good in my hand regardless. It had a sharpness and smell unlike any cheese I'd ever tasted. The secret of its creation, he said, had been in his family for over a hundred years.

Daylight was fading as I drove back down into the valley, and I stopped at a nondescript little hotel the good shepherd had told me was the only one open within twenty-five kilometers of Roquefort. A very old woman sat behind the desk, so old I assumed she would call someone from the rear when I told her I'd like a room for the night. "*Oui, monsieur,*" she answered brightly, then proceeded to register me for *une chambre* and an eight-o'clock dinner reservation with a brisk efficiency that dealt age-stereotyping a solid boot in the rear. She was ninety-one, she volunteered when I thanked her—had been born in the next village but lived numerous other places during her long life, including Paris. I told her my mother was the same age, back home in America. *Oui*, she nodded. She had known Americans during the *deuxième guerre*—"*les soldats.*" I asked her if she'd known German soldiers too, realizing only after the words fell from my lips that the question might hold for her a different, far more suggestive meaning than I'd intended. But she didn't bat an eye. "*Certainement,*" she answered. Both "*les Allemands et les Américains.*" All of them were "*corrects.*"

I was so taken by her perky charm and the modest room rate—less than forty dollars for the night—that I booked a second night on the spot, taking pains to make a dinner reservation for it too. Such polite formalities were the tiny threads that stitched the country's social fabric together, and I tried never to forget this one even when it appeared a hotel had few other guests.

Three hours later, I met the hotel's younger owners when I descended the rickety wooden staircase for the meal. A big-bellied man with a pockmarked face leaned over the bar chatting with two or three locals. His plump and carpet-slippered wife—I guessed the old woman's daughter-in-law—served as both cook and waitress in the vacant dining room at the rear. I remained its only occupant for the next two hours, savoring one of the most abundant and well-cooked dinners I'd had on the trip.

I woke the next morning to a swirling snowstorm thumping at the window, and felt even better about having booked a second night in the hotel. Lounging in bed with a Victorian novel, gazing drowsily out at the white-shrouded cliffs in the distance, I relished the snow day as shamelessly as any fifth-grader liberated from school. When the storm briefly let up around noon, I headed out for a run, pausing at the foot of the stair to chat briefly with the two women at the desk.

I told the daughter-in-law again how much I'd enjoyed her food the night before, and reconfirmed my reservation for that evening. Both women nodded and smiled. They seemed to be enjoying the day's enforced idleness as much as I was, and after a shared mock-lament on the wretched weather, I moved on toward the door. But the old woman suddenly raised a thin finger and cried out to me, as if recalling something important, the younger woman disappearing just as suddenly into the dining room. The matriarch remained at the hotel desk, her index finger now leafing slowly through the pages of a newspaper beside her discarded shawl. I had no idea why she had stopped me—what she was searching for. Finally she found it. "*Ici!,*" she cried, tapping it excitedly. Turning the page toward me, she tapped it again, an article titled "*L'eau qui fait des miracles en Aveyron.*"

I knew the Aveyron was the region I'd holed up in, but hadn't previously heard of the healing powers of its water. "*Oui,*" the old woman nodded, the gnarled finger pointing now to her eyes and her arms. "*Les yeux, la peau, les bras,*" it made no difference, she assured me, the miraculous water healed them all. I didn't ask her what part of my own aging body had stirred her to favor me with the knowledge, or whether the previous day's slog up the frigid trout stream was going to boost my virility and heal the tennis elbow that had plagued me for months. But the article's text seemed promising. The highest authorities, it read, had testified over the centuries to "*l'heureux effet*" of the "*choc psychologique*" caused by "*l'eau froide.*"

If the "shock-generating" *froideur* was what caused the promised "happy effect," I could provide my own testimony to the region's qualifications. The temperature hadn't climbed more than a degree or two above freezing since I'd left Sète. The snow started to fall again soon after I bid the old woman a fond *à bientôt* and set off on my run—continued to fall through the rest of the afternoon as I settled in once more with the novel, drifting in and out of sleep.

I woke with yet another of the trip's voracious appetites, having eaten nothing through the drowsy day but a couple of lunchtime plums. Descending the stair promptly at eight, I nodded to the easygoing *patron* slouched behind the bar and moved on toward the dining room. He stopped me a few steps from the door. "*Fermé, monsieur,*" he said nonchalantly. His wife emerged a moment later and confirmed it—"*Fermé ce soir.*" The restaurant was closed. No further word of explanation followed from either of them—merely a pair of cryptic smiles and a glowing recommendation for another restaurant in St. Affrique, twenty kilometers up the road.

The place felt as far away as Africa by the time I'd driven the icy mountain road and found it. But the food was as good as the couple had promised, and the spry old woman, back at her post when I checked out of the hotel the next morning, joined them in wishing me a *bonne journée*. We hope someday to see you again, she added cheerfully as the others nodded, walking me to the door.

If I ever pass your way in the future, *monsieur et dames*, you will.

I reflected on the experience as I drove back toward Millau the next morning and eventually found my way up to the autoroute once more. Like my frigid night in the Aniane *logis* a few nights earlier, it was one more instance of the mad twists of logic any traveler through France learns to accept as simply the way things are. I'll confess I haven't quite gotten there yet. Giving the Gallic shrug when a maze of *sortie*-pointing arrows leads you back to where you started is still beyond me. And I remain baffled by that blithe voice of French officialdom that covers everything but what you most need to know. A week later, for example, back in Paris, I arrived at the exact hour my written contract stated I was to return the car to the rental company, only to find the place locked and deserted despite the fact I'd called the day before to confirm both the date and time. The cheerful English-speaking woman on the phone had ticked off the contract details and said yes, everything was in order, they were expecting me—she was happy to learn my trip had gone well. After circling the building twice and rattling every door, I stood weighing my options for several minutes, then shrugged in bewilderment and dropped the keys in the mail slot by the entrance. Before my departure on Monday morning, I called the office again from the airport, more than a little uneasy. The same woman answered. They were closed on weekends, she informed me just as cheerfully. But everything was fine, sir, the car had been returned.

You probably didn't have to be as eccentric as I had often been accused of being to love the French, but it helped. Twice during my stay in Paris I'd walked the quarter mile from my hotel to an enticing little jazz club on the Ile St. Louis, returning both times with the slap of my shoesoles on the pavement the only beat I'd heard. On the first occasion the bartender told me the music would commence at 10:30. I left around midnight after inhaling more cigarette smoke than a piano player with a three-pack-a-day habit of Gauloise. The second time a sign in the window blared "*Tous les soirs à 21 heures. Jazz live!*" I arrived at 21:30. The place was dark and the door was barred.

At such times it helped to think of Yogi Berra. Or the French academic quoted by Adam Gopnik in his brilliant book *From Paris To The Moon*: "It will work in practice, yes. But will it work in theory?"

Fortunately, the two occasionally converged, as in the French system of marking their highways. All you needed to do was check your color-coded map to know exactly what to expect. Blue meant an autoroute—a toll-road or *péage*—where if you wanted to push the envelope you could breeze along at close to a hundred miles an hour. Green meant the same but you didn't have to pay. Red meant a "national" highway—a good road but often heavy with traffic, the French equivalent of the Highway 30's and Route 66's of my youth. And finally there were the innumerable yellow, or "D" roads like the one that had led me to Roquefort—narrow, rural byways that could be as slow as donkey trails but were nearly always the best choice if scenery and charm were what you sought. I had gotten back on the green-marked autoroute out of Millau for three reasons: the drive to Burgundy was several hundred kilometers, it had begun to snow again, and the route was toll-free.

It was also, like every Interstate or *autobahn* or *autostrada* I'd ever driven, about as boring as a road could be, the more so because it fed through one of the least picturesque parts of France. Fortunately the nation's radio programming was as dependable as its maps. With several hours of asphalt ahead of me, I flicked on the car radio to kill the time.

Finding a station was as reliable as learning the coded system of roads. Wherever you were in the country, your choices were essentially the same, nearly all of them instantly identifiable by the glowing words that flashed beside the numbers as the car's scanner scrolled across the dial. Several offered music—"*Skyrock*," "*Classique*," "*Nostalgie*," etc. A couple, "*Inter*" and "*Europe*," were more generalized but leaned toward news analysis and informed talk. And then there was the station that was almost *all* talk. Sophisticated talk. "Talk about issues that matter to you," as the Wisconsin NPR station I favored back home billed its similar programming menu. The French version was called "*France Culture*," and I'd tuned it in often enough to know the talk could literally be about anything. Still, I was unprepared for the panel discussion that filled *Culture*'s airwaves as my car rolled on toward Burgundy through the falling snow. It lasted nearly an hour. The assembled authorities were light-hearted and occasionally frivolous, but densely analytical. Their topic throughout was the timeless English expression, "Fuck-you." Or as all but one of them pronounced it, "*Fook-you*." I tried to imagine some trucker hauling ass down I-90 back home in Minnesota and chancing on the program in English. I couldn't. It was another reason why I loved France.

Four hundred kilometers and several more considerably less enlightening programs up the road I made another of the snap decisions that had come to define the trip. For an hour I'd wracked my brain trying to recall the name of Monique and Daniel's tiny hilltop hamlet, kicking myself for not writing it down before I left home. The problem wouldn't have existed if Jane and the Johnsons had been with me. Yvonne, who often lamented that she'd never forgotten anything unimportant, could have told me the place's name at once. I groped awhile longer and finally gave up. Goudou, if he hadn't shuffled off this mortal coil, would have to wait for another chance to drool on my shoes.

Pulling off the road for a longer look at the map, I made a decision whose only rationale was a quirky, trip-closing symmetry. I had the Old Shepherd's *roi de fromage* safely stowed in my trunk. What better match for it than a good *Chablis*—a wine and cheese pair known all over the world, though neither village was much larger than Guide Rock or Silver Creek. Jane and I had once spent a day in the Burgundian village and been thoroughly charmed by it, but what clinched the impetuous decision was the happy fact that a dry Chablis was my favorite white wine. The seal of approval, if one were needed, had come two days earlier during my glacial tour of the corporate cheese cave. In 1937, the verbose guide had announced proudly during one of our innumerable stops, a symbolic marriage had been performed uniting the wine of Burgundy and the regal *fromage* of Roquefort.

And so, Chablis it would be. The snow had stopped when I pulled into the little village just before nightfall, but deep furrows of slush lined the road. Many of the buildings were shuttered. I drove the empty streets for several minutes, searching for a hotel, and finally found one near the center of town. No one was at the desk, but a middle-aged woman eventually emerged from an inviting nook to the side ringed with overstuffed armchairs. Smiling warmly, she took my credit card and registered me for the night.

The first-floor *chambre* she directed me to was as patently French, and as small, as a hotel room can be. Lace curtains hung gracefully in the window. The bed was covered with a plush duvet and half a dozen embroidered pillows. A copy of Ionesco's *Rhinocéros* rested on an antique mahogany nightstand, and a polished shelf in the bathroom held a dainty wicker basket filled with scented soaps and shampoos. If the room's captivating allure didn't quite extend to the shower and toilet, I did the best Gallic shrug I could muster and ignored them. The former had sliding plastic doors so narrow and tissue-paper thin I had to turn sideways to squeeze my road-weary body through them, while the latter was outside in the hallway—a communal loo.

I ate that night in a brasserie just up the street. Three jeans-clad, athletic-looking young men sat talking at the bar when I entered, glancing up every few seconds at a tennis match on the TV. Hopping nonchalantly off his stool, the one nearest the door led me to a vacant dining room in the rear, then reappeared minutes later to take my order. Minutes more passed as I sat alone, listening to their cheers and laughter, and I finally decided to return to the bar. The young waiter smiled and nodded when he noticed. Pointing me to a table, he turned his attentions back to the screen.

The event was a Davis Cup competition between France and

Sweden, and the outcome had come down to the deciding match. I remained in the doorway for a game or two, watching and listening to the youths' running critique of the action, when the most vocal one turned suddenly toward me and asked where I was from. America, I answered him in French—a state called Minnesota.... It's where Bob Dylan was from, I added belatedly. The latter fact clearly didn't compute. "*Ah oui*," he said brightly. "*Meeneesota. Les Tamberwoolves. Kavin Garnett.*"

The grinning waiter bounced off his stool again a short time later and pointed to the bare wooden table once more. Would I prefer to eat my meal there, he asked, where I could continue to watch the match? Enjoying their company, I agreed at once and sat down. By the time France had eked out a dramatic victory, I was well into my dessert, yet remained the only diner in the place. It seemed an appropriate time—and my high-spirited companions the right age—to take advantage of the upbeat atmosphere and satisfy my curiosity. That afternoon, I said in French when the post-match celebration quieted, I'd heard a discussion on the radio of the English expression "*Fuck-you.*" The good-looking youth who had asked where I was from grinned knowingly and nodded from his perch behind the bar. The others' faces showed instant familiarity with the phrase as well.

As an American, I went on, I was curious. What did the expression mean to them? The bartender's grin widened and he flicked his middle finger at me in the air. I nodded and laughed with him. Is it *aggressif*? I asked—the kind of insult that could lead to a fight? "*Non non non*," a chorus of voices responded. He had never heard it used in that way, the bartender added. Most of the time it was just.... He stopped, shrugging his shoulders, then drove the point home with an accented flair. "*Bool-sheet,*" he said. "*Cock-sooker. Il y a beaucoup à choisir.*"

The next morning, after a fine night's sleep in the antique bed, I wedged myself in and out of the shower once more and then labored through a page or two of *Le Rhinocéros* before descending the old hotel's broad, darkly varnished stair. Again the front desk was unattended, and I walked on into the cozy breakfast nook where its only occupant, the apparent owner, greeted me with a courteous but formal air. A lean, gray-suited man in his thirties wearing a wool scarf around his long neck to ward off the chill, he directed me to the largest of the room's comfortable chairs even though I told him politely I wanted only a *café au lait*. We soon fell into an equally decorous, if somewhat stiff and tentative conversation in English as he prepared it. Chamber music played softly from a CD in the background. On a lace-covered table in the corner, half a dozen bottles of the village's distinguished *grand crus* were tastefully displayed.

Curious how such a man would respond, I raised as discreetly as I could the same question I'd asked the youths in the bar the night before. The setting was far more incongruous, but his face registered only a mild surprise. "*En general*," he shook his head sadly, "the people speak very bad. Nobody believe in God in France now. It is finished. Only the people very old."

Why do you think that is, I asked him, particularly interested in his perspective since I'd said nothing of religion, had mentioned only the crude epithet. It was some time before he answered.

"The religion is the past. Perhaps in some ways it is better," he finally said, his voice subdued.

I took a sip of the excellent coffee. The music played softly on in the silence. I took another sip and set the cup back on the saucer, a graceful piece of china propped precariously on my knees. Religious extremism was causing some terrible problems in the world, I murmured. He nodded but said nothing. Many of the most evangelically religious people in America were very distrustful of France, I added, though they often knew little about his country and didn't seem to care much about learning more.... I found that sad, I said.... *Très triste*.

The hotelier lowered his voice further, as if someone else had entered the room and he didn't want to be overheard. "*Les Américains sont très religieux*," he whispered, reverting to his native language. "*Et en même temps, très très patriotiques. C'est une contradiction.*"

Not in America, I replied. "*Le plus religieux, le plus patriotique.*"

He shook his head and whispered again that it was a contradiction to be both religious and patriotic. "*La religion et la guerre....*" he added. He stared at me as if I might be able to explain.

I took several more sips of the coffee as another long silence opened between us. When the conversation resumed it was again the hotelkeeper who raised the topic we proceeded to discuss.

"*En France tout est fini,*" he said morosely. "*Toutes les valeurs morales.*" When my eyebrows lifted he repeated it. "*Finies.*"

It was such a sweeping generalization—that all moral values were "finished" in his country—I asked him what he thought had brought about the change.

"*L'argent,*" he said. "Money. *La position sociale. Et surtout la sexualité.*" He paused to let the word sink in, then continued. "*Les mensonges*"—my brain leafed through scraps of embedded vocabulary and came up with "lying"—"*l'immoralité, l'escroquerie.*" I had no idea what the last word meant and had to check it later in my dictionary, found that it meant "swindling." "*C'est partout maintenant,*" he finished—such things were everywhere now. "*C'est très grave.*"

I asked him if he was religious.

"Yes," he responded in English. "But I am only one. No one else believe now."

The dead silence that followed felt the way a crow's or raven's does when it perches on a bough outside your window. Rising, I carefully set the cup and saucer down and thanked him, opening my wallet to pay. "*Non, monsieur,*" he said in the cheerless voice that had barely risen above a whisper the entire time we'd been talking. When a second attempt to pay for the coffee was also met with a slow shake of his head, I thanked him again and walked out into the street.

It was barely ten o'clock in the morning, but the funereal conversation and the gelid look of the shuttered village had turned my mood heavier than the soggy snow. The rash decision to revisit it in winter seemed at that moment the one truly idiotic thing I'd done on the trip. But Chablis still meant great wine, I reminded myself, regardless of the season, and a bottle of it would taste as good back in Minnesota as any bought at a leafy vineyard in June or July. I had passed several "*Cave-Dégustation*" signs the night before, driving the empty streets searching for a hotel room, and I set off now looking for one on foot.

Five minutes later I came to an ice-crusted information board clearly intended for tourists, which is exactly what I felt like at that point—a particularly feckless one at that. I might have been the first American since the World War I doughboys to have trooped down the streets of Chablis in the snow. Crunching to a stop, I was open to the smallest scrap of useful information the sign might hold.

The village produced "seven famous vintages," the crisply-lettered text read in four languages, its *grand crus* made from grapes taken from only 250 acres of land. The seven were *Preuses, Vaudésir, Bougros, Valmur, Grenouilles, Les Clos,* and *Blanchot*. Together, they formed "*les sept joyaux de la couronne.*"

My spirits lifted a little despite the weather. *Seven jewels of the crown*, one of which would go perfectly with the Old Shepherd's king of cheeses whenever I chose to consummate the Roquefort guide's gastronomic marriage with Jane and a few friends back home. I stared again at the list of vintages, something floating just outside the edge of consciousness, then suddenly burst out laughing as the realization dawned. *Grenouilles* meant "*Frogs.*" One of the seven crown jewels bore a name with a French connection even more evocative in my home country than *Chablis*. When I'd regained my bearings, I studied the sign again. It included a map of the vineyards, all seven of them only a few hundred meters from where I stood. *Grenouilles* lay closest to the river (the fact was logical enough I shouldn't have laughed again, but I did) and looked to be the smallest of the promised gems.

The irony was too rich to ignore, and I walked back to my car determined to buy a bottle of Frogs or freeze to death trying. It didn't quite come to that, but locating the vineyard proved far more difficult than I'd blithely assumed. Driving north out of the village to the spot where the map had pinpointed it, I found only unmarked, snow-blanketed rows of pruned vines.

I drove back across the ice-clogged river and resumed walking the streets, belatedly realizing that the *caves* themselves would likely be in the village itself. Still, I had no better luck for some time. Of the several wineshops I passed none carried the magic name, and I finally stopped a man on the sidewalk and asked for help. He shook his head, puzzled. No, he said, there was no such *cave* in Chablis. I mentioned the sign, repeated the uvula-strangling French word, assuming my pronunciation had been so mangled he hadn't recognized it. When his face remained clouded I half-considered croaking like a frog but decided against it. Franco-American relations were strained enough as it was.

It was not until my third or fourth attempt that I found a local who knew what I was referring to. "*Oui*," he nodded, "*Grenouilles*." But it wasn't a *cave*, he corrected me. It was a small parcel of land owned by several different *vignerons*. One of them was just around the corner. Pointing, he walked me back in the direction I had come until he was sure I could see the place a few yards up the street.

I had passed it five minutes earlier, as oblivious of the fact it was open as I'd been temporarily brain-locked on my *caves* and *crus*. Feeling even more like a *plouc*, I hastily thanked him and slouched on to the stylish little shop's glass door. It was several seconds more before I entered. The interior was so dimly lit, the lettering on the glass so discreet, it might have been the Vermeer room at the Louvre.

A beefy man in his forties stepped out of a small office to greet me, his round, keen-eyed face so disconcertingly reminiscent of Rush Limbaugh's the cockeyed quest began to feel like a voyage into the surreal. But he was as refreshingly buoyant as the hotelkeeper had been gloomy. Yes, he said, stepping away briefly to retrieve an open bottle, he had the *grand cru* I'd been searching for. Plucking a gleaming glass from under the counter, he poured me a taste. His English was almost as distinctive as the wine, and I was happy to let him fill me in on the vintage's history as he boxed the *Grenouilles* I immediately bought.

The name went back to the nineteenth century, he explained. "The people don't like to work in the vineyard because it is near the river and the frogs make the… the…." He paused, searching for the word. "Make the *croak*," he found it. "They say we don't want to go to the frog."

I laughed heartily and he did too, which widened the mutual comfort zone enough I spontaneously decided to risk a question I'd suppressed throughout the trip. "I'm sure you know that in America right now there's a lot of negative feeling about your country," I said to him. "The common anti-French term is '*Frogs*'.... I'm sure you know that too."

"Yes," he responded at once, smiling. "It is because in France we eat the frogs."

"I eat their legs myself," I hastened to assure him, "have ever since I was a boy. I used to catch them with a fishing pole and a scrap of red cloth." We both nodded in appreciation of the madcap direction the conversation had taken, laughter filling the room once more. "How do people respond to the term over here?" I said more seriously. "Is it basically something trivial, not regarded as a serious insult, or offensive to you?"

"The first, I think," he said. "But you are right, our countries do not get along now. I was in Germany one year ago to learn German. There were both Americans and French who make enroll in the class, and the teacher say he think there may be only the place for one."

This triggered another shared laugh, though mine at least was colored by the hard geopolitical realities that underlay the joke. I asked him what he thought of America's foreign policy. "Over here we think your President is a very dangerous man," he answered as so many of his countrymen before had answered me. When I told him I'd come to France at such an unseasonable time of the year largely to escape from the post-election blues, he nodded sympathetically. "We have no expression for Americans like your '*Frogs*,' I don't think," he said. "But yesterday I am watching TV and I hear someone refer to George Bush and his aides as '*peet bools*.'"

My brow wrinkled as I tried to penetrate the obscure pronunciation, and he repeated it. "Like the fighting dogs," he added helpfully. Finally I understood—*pit bulls*. He went on to say that for the past several years he had spent a couple of weeks in Egypt—developed a fondness for that country similar to what I'd told him earlier I felt for France. "Since the Iraq war the people are afraid there," he said. "It is because of the... the... the less *stability*?" He paused to check his use of the English word with me. I confirmed it and asked if he thought, from his recent trips to the Middle-Eastern country, that the terrorist threat was greater than it had been before the war. "Much greater," he said. "The war makes it all worse. The fear means that there are not so many tourists. The people become poorer. One cannot know how it is in the future, of course, but today they blame it on the United States."

When I paid for the bottle of wine and thanked him, turning to leave, he smiled and spoke some parting words. "It is best if you keep it for two years," he said, "perhaps three. Maybe to celebrate when you have a new President." We shared a final laugh and I left the store so occupied with the conversation I'd walked a block before abruptly realizing he'd never told me his name. I briefly considered walking back to ask him, but didn't. It was better simply to remember him as my French Rush, a man worth listening to.

****

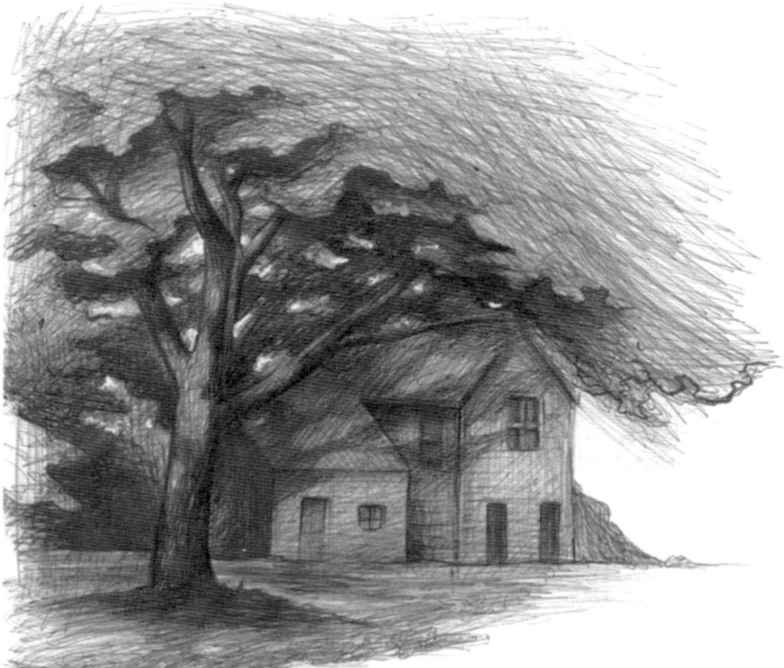

EPILOGUE

Next door to my grandmother's home, throughout my early childhood, lived an arthritic widow of indeterminate age named Mrs. Britton. She had occupied the clapboard, elm-shaded house at least as long as my widowed grandmother had occupied hers, which meant to my callow eyes that she had lived there forever. The Hansel & Gretel feel was as fixed, and unnervingly real, as the screen of hollyhocks that rose like a row of sentinels along her backyard garden, their prickly stalks edging a moldered picket fence that sagged on to eventual disintegration between the adjacent lots' almost identical pair of outhouses at the rear. If I ever saw Mrs. Britton on a Guide Rock street, or in old man Fringer's general store, it quickly faded from memory. She was an inhabitant of that cloistered house and forbidding garden alone.

Hearing the rasp of her hoe, I'd creep faint-heartedly up to the worn patch of grass where a slight gap in the thicket of flowers afforded a covert view of her—a small, bent woman in an ankle-length dress and high-topped black shoes, her face barely visible beneath the tunnel-like brim of her sunbonnet. I knew almost nothing about her, beyond those clandestinely observed details and her fondness for organ music. More than once, tossing a football or baseball in my grandmother's yard, I stopped frozen in my tracks by a sudden peal of it piercing the air, then crept to the fence hoping, and half fearing, to glimpse her life's shadowy interior through the back-door screen.

I never did. An unfiltered view of small-town America in those middle years of the last century emerged only through another next-door dwelling, this one in Silver Creek, where no fringe of flowers could obscure the muted pain. Inhabited by a crippled woman in a urine-smelling wheelchair and her alcoholic son, their ramshackle house was my first exposure to the quiet desolation that would later, under harsher economic conditions, engulf the blighted prairie ghost towns where makeshift methamphetamine labs were the only growth industry.

The latter woman's name was Mrs. Roth, her deathly pale and wasted son's, Harvey Leith, the bewildering non-conformity of their last names only one of several obscure and disturbing things that made their lives as charged with mystery as Mrs. Britton's. The jarring difference was that in their case I saw all too much of what lay behind the creaking, oilcloth-covered back door. Once or twice a month, my mother would make up two extra plates of food for their supper, or Mrs. Roth would call over to ask if someone could cash a ten-dollar money order for her at the Post Office downtown. In either case I was the delivery boy, and the sights and smells of their cramped, fly-specked kitchen—the only part of the house I ever entered—remain unforgettable to this day: the overpowering odor of cooking cabbage; Mrs. Roth's swollen-knuckled hands twisted like gnarled roots on her wheelchair; Harvey's unmade cot glimpsed in a side room, the sheets smeared with stains I averted my eyes not to see. Into my otherwise harmonic world they intruded like the rasp of an untuned fiddle, or the passed-out Harvey's emaciated body splayed on the gravel road between our houses like a pile of broken sticks.

Nostalgia for the "strong, pungent, and exotic flavors" of that faded culture is tempered, in short, by an acute awareness that the flavors were often far from benign. And though I had found my latest trip abroad immensely fulfilling, it had only deepened my awareness that the fact was as true of *la France profonde* as it has always been of the United States. The European country's local colors remained enduringly vivid for me, even in the winter. But its vulnerability to the same socioeconomic forces that had withered rural America was no less apparent, a hard truth visible to eyes keener than mine as far back as the 1950's, when the French director Claude Chabrol filmed his moving tale of rural fatalism and despair, *Le Beau Serge*. Set in the Creuse region of southwest France near Limousin, the film's isolated village is about as far as life can get from Mayberry.

Viewing it again after my return home, I found the movie almost as sobering as *Mondovino*—a pointed reminder that however much one might long to, romanticizing the Dordogne or Languedoc at some personally idyllic point in their history was as out of touch with reality as stopping the clock in Middle America back when "you could feel the old world go and the new one beginning," as Bob Dylan has aptly described that vanished age.

"France has a very dark side," a Minnesota friend said to me not long ago, in the wake of the incendiary protest marches and random acts of violence that had swept the country in the months after my return. That she was French, a native of Paris, lent her words a potency reinforced by other, equally penetrating voices from both sides of the Atlantic in the protests' aftermath. France was a society that "no longer knew how to create the dream of a better life for its new generations," wrote the French novelist Antoine Audouard. The opposition that led French voters to reject a new European Union constitution, observed Adam Gopnik, was in part "irrational and racist—based on a fear of East European workers taking the jobs of French ones, and of Turks overwhelming Europeans in the E. U." And in an especially chilling excerpt from his book profiling Osama bin Laden, the former *Washington Post* correspondent Jonathan Randal quoted the words of a brilliant young Paris engineering student, the son of Algerian immigrants, who grew up in one of the dead-end suburban projects where the Muslim riots flared. It was his sudden awakening to "the abominable treatment meted out to all the potential 'myselves' who had been conditioned to become subcitizens good only to keep working to pay for the retirement of the 'real' French," the youth testified, that opened him to Al Qaeda's jihadist call.

There is a very dark side to France. Watching the televised images of burning cars and angry, chanting young Islamist men from the seclusion of my Minnesota home—the glazed faces of impotent Elysée bureaucrats voicing mealy-mouthed platitudes—I thought of the individuals I'd met a few brief months earlier. Tried to imagine their reactions staring at the same televised scenes, hitting so much closer to home. Despite the contacts I'd made with them, I couldn't. Where was Benchabane, the devout young Muslim waiter I'd met in Lodève who had given such frank, incisive answers to my probing questions? What were France and Michel Dols saying to one another, in the quiet safety of their vineyard near St. Cirq-Lapopie? And what of the aristocratic old vintner Aimé Guibert, with his fierce integrity and social conscience—or the outspoken Alex and her keen-eyed boyfriend in Souillac—or the two aged couples, their long lives marked by the horrific sights and sounds of D-Day, contemplating this latest *déluge de feu* from their pristine houses tucked behind protective walls in Arromanches?

It was impossible to know what any of them were thinking or feeling—perhaps *doing*—as their nation experienced social upheavals of a magnitude not seen since the late 1960's, any more than all those years ago I knew the dark realities masked by Harvey Leith's slack, deer-in-the-headlights smile. Mental images flickered of countless others as well—remembered individuals from two far-flung rural cultures whose lives had intersected mine through more than sixty years of life and travel. The only thing I felt confident of, without a trace of literary irony, was that they were good country people, nearly all of them, and I remained as trusting of their best instincts as they had so often shown their trust in mine.

Five years earlier, on the most frigid winter night I'd known in the three decades I had lived in Minnesota, I'd had an experience that would come to crystallize for me what a culture risks losing when its small farms and villages die. By dusk the raw temperature had fallen to twenty degrees below zero, the wind chill closer to seventy. Over Jane's strenuous objections, I decided it was imperative to drive the thirty miles down to our cabin in the woods to drain the water pipes, convinced that otherwise they would freeze and burst as they'd done during a less severe cold front three years before. Though the cabin was essentially mine alone, a secluded retreat for writing and various outdoor activities, Jane had gamely pulled on her coat to go with me before I finally convinced her the job required only one set of hands and less than five minutes to perform. Briefly quieting her mounting anxieties, I pulled on my coat and gloves and set off into the squall.

The road out of town was icy and windswept, buffeted with frequent gusts that shook the car so violently I was several times on the edge of turning back over the next half-hour, spurred on only by the dread of dealing with water-sogged wallboards and floors. I worried most about a steep hill ten miles from the cabin, a stretch of switchback curves with no guardrail snaking steeply down to the valley carved by a trickling stream below. That harrowing descent behind me, I would have only relative flatland to navigate the rest of the way to my remote patch of ground. Reaching the hill's crest, I slowed to an uneasy stop, then crept on down the glazed blacktop until I felt my knuckles finally loosen on the steering wheel and my lungs refill with air after the longest mile I'd ever traversed.

The momentary lapse of concentration could easily have been the last of my life. Though my now slightly accelerated speed remained well under thirty miles an hour, it was too fast for glare ice, and I was propelled almost at once into a roadside to roadside shimmy that ended with the car abruptly airborne, its headlights flashing surrealistically over cattails and the shallow creek. I didn't lose consciousness in the shock that followed, a metal-shearing jolt that had the brutal finality of a headlong smash into a brick wall, but the sudden silence sustained the hallucinatory imagery of a bad dream. The car had come to rest on the concrete remains of a bridge abutment. A rusted girder impaled the back seat, the ice-choked creek flowing sluggishly on several feet below the car's axles. The passenger seat—Jane's seat had she come with me—lay compressed under the crumpled door.

Remarkably, my only injuries were a nosebleed and what later proved to be a cracked rib from the slam of my upper body into the steering wheel. Shuddering less from the pain spearing my chest than the nightmarish vision of the unoccupied seat next to me, I opened my own undamaged door and jumped down into the frigid water, ice shattering under my feet.

What followed in the next few minutes would not strike most people in my rural township as particularly notable, which may say more about the experience than words can. The accident had happened directly across the road from a barnyard, less than fifty yards from where a parka-hooded dairyman was fork-lifting a tractor load of hay to his cows. It was apparent he'd neither seen nor heard the crash in the howling wind. Clambering unsteadily up the stream bank, I crossed the road behind him and hobbled on toward the house where a lamp glowed through a curtained window, the occupied farmer still oblivious that a shaken stranger now stood at his door.

The woman who answered my knock stood for a moment simply staring at me, her stunned gaze drifting from my bloodied face down to my mud-coated boots. I briefly described what had happened, asked if I could use their telephone to call my wife back in Winona and the highway patrol. She opened the door at once and ushered me on into the kitchen. Sometime during the next twenty minutes, as I reassured Jane that I was all right and gave the county sheriff the specifics of the accident and its location, her husband finished his chores and entered the room. When I hung up and turned back to thank them, we made our belated introductions, and he asked where I'd been heading on such a brutal night. I told him. Without a moment's hesitation, his wife nodding her vigorous assent, the grizzled farmer lifted his car keys off a hook and handed them to me. "Take ours," he said. "It's parked just outside the back door."

I returned from France as the first, faint signs of spring were beginning to emerge along the upper Mississippi. The ice was breaking up on the river. The aspens and birches had not yet begun to green on the hillsides, but that would come soon, as would the subtler shades of fiddlehead ferns and Dutchman's breeches—the pungent smell of morels popping out of the earth under dying elms. It was a good time to be home.

But it was good too to have been away, let the winter angst drain from my soul. Nothing I'd experienced abroad had diminished my love of France. But I was an American, with ties to a rural culture that had only grown stronger through its slow decline under economic realities that were often, but not always, inevitable as the passing of time. I continued to admire the French for their resistance to those that weren't—the keen sense of injustice that, scarcely a year later, would link the nation's students and farmers and union workers in a country-wide collective protest against the growing economic *précarité* and corporate globalization threatening their traditional way of life. Reflexively condemned by outsiders as "a reactionary or even Luddite position," a "sterile popular defense of an obsolete social and economic order," as the Parisian columnist William Pfaff astutely observes in a recent essay, the massive demonstrations were from a more penetrating perspective a voice crying in the wilderness, an anxious canary in the mine. From this vantage point, in the words of the social critic Philippe Grasset, the millions of French in the streets had mounted a passionate challenge to the widely heard plea that France "cease to set itself off by its taste for what is passé... its old-fashionedness." How many of us, nostalgic visitors from other shores, I wondered, had come to share this visceral distrust of the corporate moneymen's smug mantra—their globalist assumption that the stiffbacked nation must "adapt to the new conditions," like it or not?

Too little of that sense of skepticism and outrage remained in my own country, I concluded unhappily, which at least partly explained the Gallic survival of a rural culture such as America had once known but no longer did. Not at least as it continued to be known, and beloved, in France. The challenge for a wistful American freshly home from a journey back in time was to avoid being so dazzled by it he failed to appreciate what remained of vibrant country life in his own land.

For there were surviving pockets, if I looked around me, even some emerging springs of hope. The little village nearest my cabin had recently completed a ten-year communal effort that had brought a nature center and extended bike trail to the region. Thirty miles farther on up the abandoned railbed where the trail had been laid, a slightly larger village boasted several thriving family-owned businesses, a trio of small restaurants nearly as good as those in the French campagne, and a professional theater with an annual Ibsen festival that celebrated the area's Norwegian heritage. Twenty minutes closer lay a wooded valley owned by counter-culture survivors from the Sixties, men and women who had turned their own tiny plots of land into organic farms and plant nurseries much as the Dols had done with their viniculture in Quercy. I saw several of them whenever Jane and I attended a foreign movie at the Winona Film Society, which their collective efforts had helped create, and at a small farmers' market brightened by its own distinctive local tints of the *terroir*. If such things had not yet come to the villages of my childhood, it was too soon to give up on them. A recent letter from a friend in Nebraska spoke of the gradual spread of organic weed control and rotational grazing, of recycled farm wastes and an open market where a day earlier he'd bought a locally grown free-range chicken and a first-rate chèvre. Rural values died hard, hard as the sandburs and burdock rooted in the prairie. I knew no more of what the future might hold than I'd known all those years ago of Mrs. Britton, listening to the haunting strains of her organ music drift faintly across her flower garden to my ear.

ACKNOWLEDGMENTS

It's unfortunately not possible to thank all of the many individuals whose values and generosity have shaped this book from its first stirrings in the rural Nebraska of my childhood to the experiences in France that grew into an embryonic draft two years ago. In the absence of these more specific words of gratitude, I want to thank collectively the good people of Silver Creek and Guide Rock, Nebraska; Houston, Minnesota; and the numerous Frenchmen and Frenchwomen whose kindness and hospitality will warm my memories of their country for the rest of my life. Several of the latter are mentioned by name in the preceding pages, among them Pierre Affre and his family in Paris; the Messieurs and Mesdames Duchez and Marot in Arromanches-les-Bains; Monique, Jean-Paul, Yann, Romaine, and the vibrant young expatriate Alexandra in Souillac; Michel and France Dols in Bouzies; my radiant cuisine-advisor Estelle in Cahors; Monsieur Vincent, le Président, in Lalbenque; the poet winemaker Aimé Guibert and his accommodating assistant Lydia in Aniane; the wry "pope" Pius of St. Saturnin and his delightful wife and daughters; the insightful young waiter Benchabane in Lodève; and two unforgettable individuals whose names I neglected to ask: the spry, nonagenarian innkeeper outside Roquefort, and the droll vintner, my French Rush, in Chablis.

Of the many who furthered the book's long evolution from the early glimmer of an idea to publication, special thanks to Jim Armstrong and Yvonne Johnson for their painstaking input on style and subject matter; and to Paul Olson, Chris Livingston, Lew and Pamela Hunter, Jay Parini, Scott Bestul, Bruce Johnson, Ed Hahn, Joe Jackson, Kathleen Starostka, Jim and Ann Nichols, Mark Breneman, Ryan Meier, Ladette Randolph, Joe and Barb Kolupke, and the dedicated staffs of the Winona State University and Winona public libraries for their many contributions to my life and work. I'm deeply indebted as well to my dear and longtime friends in our Winona book club—the Johnsons, Kiihnes, Lunds, Meekers, and Stevens—for their unfailing encouragement and gentility; to Francesca Giambartolomei and Elvira Lanciotti for their excellent advice on European publishing contacts; to Nick Tolimieri, Quentin Tolimieri, and Jessica Gaynor for their stimulating companionship; to my colleagues at Winona State University for the supportive, collegial environment they fostered; and profoundly, to the following people: my publisher, Bernard Cesari, whose courageous decision to publish the book in English is a debt far too large for words to repay; Rosine Tenenbaum, for her polished, eye-opening French translation, which has illuminated aspects of the work I wasn't aware of; and the artistic staff at Ibis Press for the superb illustrations that grace the work.

Love and boundless appreciation also to the members of my family: my brothers and lifelong soul-mates, Doug and Scott; my sisters-in-law Carol and Nancy, cousins Lila Lee Tobey and Madeline Rasmuson and their husbands David and Nelson; my seven lively nieces and nephews; my lovely daughter-in-law Kari Cooper; and especially my mother Barbara, peerless caregiver and nurturer, and my aunt Donna Crosley, whose clarity of mind and quiet benevolence have so long fortified me. Closer to home, I want to thank my wife Jane for qualities far too numerous to mention. Her longsuffering patience with the personal quirks visible on virtually every page of this memoir is rivaled only by her invaluable intellectual contributions to the book.

And finally, to my beloved sons Eric and Andy, my gratitude for the countless ways you continue to sustain me, and sincere apologies for the shortcomings apparent here, both of life and of art. The great pilgrimage poet's keen aphorism, "The lyf so short, the craft so long to lerne", has lost none of its edge since Chaucer first articulated it hundreds of years ago. Only in the silent dance of memory and imagination, alas, can we find ourselves truly back in time.